In God We Trust

George Schwartz (signature)

GEORGE P. SCHWARTZ, CFA
with MICHAEL O. KENNEY, JD

foreword by LOU HOLTZ

TAN
Charlotte, North Carolina

Cover design by Greg Malcolm

ISBN: 978-1-5051-1346-4

Library of Congress Control Number: 2018958391

Published in the United States by
TAN Books
PO Box 410487
Charlotte, NC 28241
www.TANBooks.com

Printed in the United States of America

For Judi Pearl – The Wind Beneath My Wings

CONTENTS

ACKNOWLEDGEMENTS.. 1

FOREWORD BY COACH LOU HOLTZ... 3

INTRODUCTION 5

Why Morally Responsible Investing?

    CHAPTER 1 – Faith, Friends, & Funds................................ 9

    CHAPTER 2 – The Heart of the Matter............................. 22

    CHAPTER 3 – A Lifetime Preparing 36

    CHAPTER 4 – Abortion 53

    CHAPTER 5 – Pornography... 67

How Does This Work?

    CHAPTER 6 – Morally Responsible Investing 89

    CHAPTER 7 – Faith & Reason 106

    PHOTO GALLERY 124

    CHAPTER 8 – A Clear Principle of Wisdom....................... 136

    CHAPTER 9 – Good Returns 161

What Are the Next Steps?

    CHAPTER 10 – From Many One..................................... 169

    CHAPTER 11 – Sound Advice 192

    CHAPTER 12 – In Memoriam....................................... 207

    CHAPTER 13 – The Best Way Forward 220

APPENDIX A – *In God We Trust* BY MICHAEL NOVAK................. 242

APPENDIX B – Discussion Questions 253

REGULATORY LEGAL DISCLOSURES...................................... 260

INDEX... 262

ACKNOWLEDGEMENTS

In 2001, my friends Tom Monaghan and Bowie Kuhn provided the inspiration and support for me to start the Ave Maria Mutual Funds. At that time, I never dreamed our mutual fund complex would grow to its present size of over $2.2 billion in assets with 100,000+ shareholders. Tom did, however, because he is a genuine visionary. It is now the largest family of Catholic mutual funds in the country. Tom has been enormously successful in numerous business and philanthropic endeavors, including Domino's Pizza, Detroit Tigers, Ave Maria University, Legatus, Spiritus Sanctus Academies, Ave Maria School of Law, Ave Maria Radio, and building the cathedral in Nicaragua. An outspoken and passionate advocate for the unborn, Tom has had a gigantic positive influence on my life, especially spiritually.

My career in managing investments has spanned 50 years. During that time, I have worked with many fine individuals. Early in my career, I was blessed with the influence of my father, Walter G. Schwartz, my mother, Marian V. Schwartz and my brother, Gregory J. Schwartz. Over those same 50 years, my wife, Judi, has been a pearl of great value and the guiding light of my life.

I started Schwartz Investment Counsel, Inc. in 1980. Richard L. Platte, Jr. is the President and has been with the firm since 1987. Rick is a brilliant, hard-working colleague and friend, who is the most well-read person I know. He also helped edit this book. Additionally, all five of my children, Annie, Mike, Tim, Bob and Katie are employed at the firm. What a joy it is to work with these highly-educated and talented individuals. We also have many other gifted analysts, portfolio managers and operations people, who make up an incredible team of professionals, all of whom take their fiduciary responsibility very seriously.

After my last book was published in 2010 – *Good Returns, Making Money by Morally Responsible Investing* – I was sure my book-writing days were over. It's hard to write a book, at least for me it is, especially while running a mutual fund management firm. If not for my collaborator, Michael Kenney, this book would never have come together. He is a gifted writer, educator, and attorney. This book started out as simply an updated version, or a second edition of *Good Returns*. But at the suggestion and with the enormous help of my colleague and son Bob Schwartz, *In God We Trust* goes much deeper into the subject of Morally Responsible Investing.

George P. Schwartz, CFA

JULY 2018

FOREWORD

One of my favorite sayings is, "Nothing on this earth is standing still. It's either growing or it's dying." *In God We Trust* chronicles a growing movement of investors who seek to persuade corporate America to adopt policies that respect the dignity of every human being from the moment of conception. Eight years ago, I wrote the foreword to *Good Returns,* the book that introduced the concept of Morally Responsible Investing. I'm pleased to be a part of this sequel. As you will see, this remarkable story continues to unfold with impressive results.

In this easy to read book, you will learn how Schwartz Investment Counsel, Inc. identifies high performing companies that do not participate in, contribute to, or support abortion or pornography. This is an inspiring story filled with practical advice and wise insights.

In 2001, George Schwartz, CEO of Schwartz Investment Counsel, Inc., together with Tom Monaghan, founder of Domino's Pizza, and the late Bowie Kuhn, former Commissioner of Major League Baseball, launched a series of investment vehicles known as the Ave Maria Mutual Funds. These funds provide investors with an opportunity to invest in a manner consistent with their faith.

When George's firm invests in a company, he sends a letter to the company's CEO emphasizing that Ave Maria Mutual Funds invested in the shares of that company because of its strong investment merits and because of its absence of ties to abortion and pornography. The letter concludes that if these attributes cease to exist, the shares will be sold. I admire this clarity and professional candor.

George, a life-long Catholic (and a big Notre Dame fan), is a registered investment adviser with a half century of investment experience. George has done an outstanding job of growing these pro-life mutual funds, which now exceed $2 billion in assets, with a serious effort that comes from a deep moral commitment. He and his team have a great work ethic (teamwork and work ethic are things I know something about). These guys have a sophisticated investment approach, and they are highly focused. They don't spend much time on the golf course — no time for that. In one of my own books, *Wins, Losses, and Lessons,* I wrote, "I would never hire a guy who keeps golf clubs in the trunk of his car." George doesn't — believe me, I've played with him — perhaps that's why the investment performance has been so good. George and his team of professionals have made a lot of money for me personally through the Ave Maria Mutual Funds and they've done it in a morally responsible way.

Lou Holtz

JULY 2018

INTRODUCTION

Wise investment management is a moral imperative. Why? Because prudent investing is essential to meeting future needs and community needs, particularly through charitable giving. But there is another, perhaps more subtle moral dimension. When we invest in a company, we become an owner, and our investment contributes to the company's success. Are we comfortable with what we own? Does the enterprise reflect our core beliefs? If not, what opportunities exist to invest in a manner that does reflect these beliefs?

This book is about participating in the capital markets in a purposeful, reasoned, and ethical way to achieve legitimate investment objectives and avoid morally objectionable businesses. In these pages, I will acquaint you with an approach to prudent and profitable investing that can help provide for your future, accumulate reserves for charitable giving, and achieve other financial objectives.

Investing is a critical component of financial management carrying with it the obligations of productivity and the exercise of sound judgment. My methods are based on well-established investment practices that are ethically valid, entirely practical, and financially astute. I will include real life investing outcomes to illustrate my assertions.

It would be silly to claim that only good, moral, and religious people can succeed at investing. There are numerous examples of dirty rotten scoundrels who have made killings in the stock market. Yet, there is a

relationship between conviction in spiritual matters and acumen in ana-
lyzing investment opportunities. That relationship lies primarily in two
areas: (1) an ability to see beyond surface features; and (2) a willingness
to dedicate oneself to disciplined practices over time.

By what authority do I offer advice on morality? I am not a priest,
rabbi, or theologian. I'm a grateful Catholic convinced by the truth,
beauty, and goodness of the Catholic Church. While I do not speak
for the Church, I draw from the Catholic intellectual tradition and the
Judeo-Christian tradition.

My primary credential for offering advice on Morally Responsible
Investing is that with the help of my colleagues and the Catholic
Advisory Board, my firm started and manages the Ave Maria Mutual
Funds — the world's largest family of Catholic mutual funds, now
exceeding $2 billion in assets. The Catholic Advisory Board consists
of individuals distinguished by their commitment to truth, excellence,
and the Catholic Faith.

AVE MARIA MUTUAL FUNDS

There are five different mutual funds, each with a particular investment focus:

Ave Maria Value Fund – AVEMX (MAY, 2001)
(formerly Ave Maria Catholic Values Fund)
*Companies believed to be undervalued relative to
their intrinsic worth.*

Ave Maria Growth Fund – AVEGX (MAY, 2003)
*Mid-cap and larger companies offering above-average potential
for growth in revenues, profits, and cash flow.*

Ave Maria Bond Fund – AVEFX (MAY, 2003)
*Domestic investment-grade debt of government and
corporate issuers and may invest up to 20% of its assets
in equity securities.*

Ave Maria Rising Dividend Fund – AVEDX (MAY, 2005)
*Common stocks of companies with a long history of
increasing dividends.*

Ave Maria World Equity Fund – AVEWX (APRIL, 2010)
Companies of all capitalizations from around the world.

These mutual funds take a pro-life, pro-family approach to investing. We only invest in companies that do not violate core teachings of the Catholic Church as set forth by the Catholic Advisory Board. In particular, the Funds screen out companies that support abortion or pornography.

THE MORAL HIGH GROUND

The moral imperative of wise investment management demands that we conduct our financial lives with the understanding that in all we do, we stand under the watchful eye of God. In the words of Pope Benedict XVI, "every economic decision has a moral consequence."[1] If you sense that the arguments I put before you are true, then I urge you to consider what they imply for your own investing.

Having talented, experienced investment professionals along with perseverance, patience, and perspective provides the basis for solid investment returns. This has been our experience.

George P. Schwartz, CFA

JULY 2018

CHAPTER I

FAITH, FRIENDS,
& FUNDS

God sends us friends to be our firm support in the
whirlpool of struggle. In the company of friends we will
find strength to attain our sublime ideal.

— ST. MAXIMILIAN KOLBE

I may be the world's most enthusiastic proponent of Morally Responsible Investing, but I have to admit that MRI was not my idea. There have been times during my career when I did not purchase a certain stock because I disliked the firm's practices (there were other times when I held my nose and bought anyway, because the numbers were just too attractive to ignore). But I had never tried to combine securities analysis with moral judgment in any systematic way.

I was skeptical about funds created for the purpose of investing "responsibly." For me, social responsibility and stock market returns were two distinctly different issues. I held the common view that a company's duty is to deliver profit to its shareholders, who are free to support whatever charitable initiatives or social objectives they like — one having nothing to do with the other.

That view was challenged in a serious way one morning in January of 2001. Tom Monaghan, the well-known businessman and philan-

thropist, invited me to a meeting at the headquarters of the Ave Maria
Foundation, an organization he had established to pursue his interest in
Catholic education and evangelism. Bowie Kuhn, former Commissioner
of Major League Baseball and a Catholic layman active in a wide variety
of Church-related projects, also attended. I had managed investments
for both of these gentlemen over the years, and had always admired
their commitment to our shared faith and the causes that touched their
hearts. They put a proposition to me which at first left me quite confused. They wanted me to start a Catholic mutual fund.

"What exactly is a Catholic mutual fund?" I asked.

While I was aware that funds with religious affiliations existed, I
had never been involved with one. In what kinds of companies would a
Catholic mutual fund invest — firms that made religious goods, (cru-
cifixes, rosaries and the like), or publishers of Bibles and catechetical
books, or construction companies that specialized in building churches
and parochial schools?

The concept of "Catholic investing" seemed rather limited. Tom
and Bowie found my befuddled expression quite amusing. They had
both been serving on the advisory board of a fund called the Catholic
Values Investment Trust. CVIT had assets of about $30 million under
management, a large portion of which was Tom's money. While it was
supposed to reflect "Catholic values," its managers selected investments
according to criteria typical of most "socially responsible" funds. Unfortunately, "socially responsible" too often includes practices inconsistent
with core Catholic teachings, particularly those that concern the dignity
of the human person.

Tom and Bowie noticed that the people running CVIT tended to waive the "Catholic values" restrictions for attractive stocks. This did not sit well with them. They roughed out the idea of a fund in which anyone (Catholics or non-Catholics) could invest that would examine stocks from the specific perspective of Catholic moral teaching. Tom and Bowie wanted to invest in the best companies in any field, but screen out firms supporting abortion or pornography.

Their idea was both thought-provoking and challenging. In so many words, they said: If you understand how destructive abortion and pornography are to our social fabric, what are you prepared to do about it?

- You could make a placard and walk up and down the street.
- You could put up a billboard or buy time on a radio station.
- You could give money to pro-life and anti-pornography organizations.

But how much could you really hope to accomplish by individual action? On the other hand, if you got a group of like-minded, motivated people together, what could they accomplish collectively?

- They could channel their resources into a mutual fund, since we live in a capitalistic society.
- They could influence corporate behavior through investing, and choose where and where not to invest.

As a group, they would have much more impact — possibly a

significant impact. An interesting premise—even if it struck me as rather overly optimistic. I didn't dismiss the idea out of hand, however. Instead, I threw a couple thoughts of my own back at them:

- Changing corporate behavior is a laudable goal, but it seems to me that such an objective would have to be pretty far down the road.
- Starting from scratch, you would need a more modest and clearly defined mission.
- Still, a fund such as they were suggesting could at least give people a means to invest in a manner consistent with their faith.

These thoughts reframed the idea in a way I could grasp.

It is essential to have well defined criteria for selecting stocks. Faith, particularly Catholic faith, provides well defined precepts. A fund based on Catholic moral philosophy — that vast and elaborate edifice of scholarship and wisdom constructed over centuries and validated by the Magisterium (teaching authority) of the Church — provides ample substance, clarity, and legitimacy. The clear, concise teaching of the Catholic Faith could be a practical and manageable basis for decision-making.

By contrast, ideology-driven "socially responsible" funds lack clear investing parameters. Expressions of broad, generalized intent such as "saving the planet" or "creating equal opportunity" or "ending exploitation" or any other amorphous, nebulous objective invites interpretation. This leads to inconsistency.

A fund that only invested in companies that did not support abortion or pornography began to seem doable and certainly quite intriguing, particularly given my respect for Tom Monaghan and Bowie Kuhn. These are men of integrity committed to defending the unborn and to building a culture of life where the exploitation of the human person is unthinkable and intolerable.

ADVENTURES WITH TOM

I first met Tom in 1976 through my wife, Judi. She had gotten acquainted with him at the University of Notre Dame, where they were both part of a group that had come from Ann Arbor, Michigan, to participate in a retreat on campus. Tom had achieved regional celebrity status because of his success with Domino's Pizza, the food-service company he'd founded a decade-and-a-half earlier. During a dinner Tom was hosting for all the retreatants (at a pizza parlor near Notre Dame, since he made it a practice to check out the competition), Judi happened to mention that her husband was an investment counselor. This apparently piqued Tom's interest, and he said he'd like to meet me.

An opportunity presented itself soon after, when Judi and I ran into him at a fund-raiser for Ann Arbor's Father Gabriel Richard Catholic High School. Judi introduced us, and we got into an extended chat. I was surprised at how similar our views were on a range of topics. We were both practicing Catholics and both Republicans, intolerant of the liberalism that we agreed was "spreading like a cancer" throughout society. Both of us were sports enthusiasts; in 1984, Tom would buy the Detroit Tigers baseball team. In essence, we hit it off right from the start. Thus began a long and fruitful association.

Some years later, Tom would invite me to attend the weekly breakfasts held at Domino's Farms, headquarters of his pizza company, hosted by a Catholic men's group. The Tuesday-morning gatherings began with 7:00 a.m. Mass and included guest breakfast speakers addressing various topics of inspirational interest. I found the presentations engaging and the camaraderie of fellow Catholic men uplifting (and still attend as often as I can).

Even the setting was interesting. In contrast to its rustic name, Domino's Farms is a thoroughly modern, architecturally distinctive, and huge (almost one million square feet in space and nearly a kilometer in length) multi-tenant office park, designed in the famous "Prairie Style" of Frank Lloyd Wright. The farm aspect is provided by the surroundings, which include fields under active cultivation and rolling pastures populated by specialty breeds of cattle along with a herd of North American bison. There's also Domino's Petting Farm, an agricultural exhibition and teaching facility that draws families and school groups from around the area.

The pairing of rural life and Frank Lloyd Wright reflects Tom's interests and personal history. Long a Wright enthusiast, Tom had wanted to be an architect before being lured onto a different path by the pizza business, and he spent part of his childhood living on a farm.

My contacts with Tom continued both in and out of the men's breakfasts. Over the years, I had numerous opportunities to watch him in action, both in his business dealings and in his personal relationships. I was impressed with his kindness and generosity, and benefited from it myself. Once in 1992, he made arrangements for me to use his personal box at Detroit's Tiger Stadium to entertain some clients. He had just sold the team to Mike Ilitch, founder of the rival pizza chain, Little Caesar's. This was, in fact, the very last night the box was under Tom's control. My clients and I were treated royally, fed to bursting with Domino's products, which the waiter who served us explained made us something of a footnote in Detroit baseball history. This was the last time Domino's Pizza would be served. Beginning the next day, the fare would be Little Caesar's.

As it happened, a short time after that experience, Harry Silverman, Domino's Pizza Vice President of Finance, called me about looking into some investments, both for the pizza company and for Tom personally. I made an appointment for Harry to come to my firm's headquarters. On the day of our appointment, he showed up with two colleagues, Paul Roney, who then was treasurer of Domino's, and Mike Marcantonio, a CPA and tax specialist for the company. The three toured our offices, meeting all of my analysts and portfolio managers. They asked extensive questions about our investment philosophy, our track record, and how we might be able to help Tom and Domino's with their investment needs. They must have been impressed with what they learned because a week later, they transferred a multi-million-dollar portfolio to Schwartz Investment Counsel, Inc. My firm has managed investments for the Monaghan Family ever since.

During the 1980s and early '90s, Tom had become increasingly immersed in charitable activities, especially projects involving the Church. He founded Legatus, the international Catholic business leaders' fraternal organization, established private Catholic elementary schools in the Ann Arbor area and mission schools in Central America, and underwrote construction of a new cathedral in Managua,

Nicaragua, to replace one that had been destroyed in an earthquake. Also in those years, Domino's was experiencing a series of wild fluctuations in its business fortunes. It nearly collapsed in 1992, then recovered dramatically, under Tom's renewed focus, and over the next six years achieved some of its greatest successes.

The stresses of business were beginning to weigh on Tom, and he became more and more drawn to faith-related endeavors. So much so that he decided to sell Domino's. In 1998, Tom accepted an offer of approximately $1 billion in a leveraged buyout from the private equity firm Bain Capital (at the time, run by Mitt Romney).

Such a substantial infusion of cash gave Tom the wherewithal to let his charitable instincts run wild, and a series of innovative, Catholic-themed start-ups and acquisitions soon followed in rapid succession. Tom founded Ave Maria Institute, a post-secondary school that was the first step in the development of Ave Maria College and later, Ave Maria University. He hired a former Michigan public prosecutor, Richard Thompson, who had gained fame for his battle with physician-assisted suicide advocate, Jack Kevorkian (the notorious "Dr. Death"), to start the Thomas More Law Center, a Catholic public-interest law firm specializing in pro-life and religious-liberty issues. He then lured Bernard Dobranski, dean of the law school at Catholic University of America, away from that venerable institution to start Ave Maria School of Law in Ann Arbor.

Casting his philanthropic net over a wide stretch of Catholic life, Tom acquired an interest in Catholic Singles Online, a digital matchmaking service, changing the name to Ave Maria Singles. He bought and invested in several Michigan AM radio stations and started Ave

Maria Radio, a media-communications firm that is now the leading source of original Catholic radio programming in the nation (and a major program provider to the EWTN Global Catholic Radio service, the audio arm of Mother Angelica's Eternal Word Television Network). And there was much more, including the underwriting of a new order of nuns, the Dominican Sisters of Mary, Mother of the Eucharist, to operate the Catholic elementary schools he funded (that order has since become one of the fastest-growing communities of Religious women in the world).

Subsequent years have seen several of his undertakings succeed brilliantly. Some have had their day and faded into the mists of lay Catholic history. With Tom's multi-faceted business background, his track record of faith-based entrepreneurship, and his activist bent, it made sense that he would eventually see investing as a vehicle to make a positive impact on behalf of unborn children and Catholic values.

THE BOWIE FACTOR

Bowie Kuhn had an undeniable cachet. He was well known, well liked, and recognized both in and out of the sports world, even long after he had retired from baseball. I remember walking down 42nd Street in New York with Bowie and his wife, Luisa. People would wave and call out, "How ya doin', Commish! What do you think of the Yankees' chances this year?" (by then, he hadn't been Baseball Commissioner for over 20 years). Bowie was always generous with his time. He'd stop and talk to strangers, give autographs, discuss baseball. He had a photographic memory capable of recalling games, and even specific plays, that had occurred 30 or 40 years before.

Bowie served as Commissioner of Major League Baseball from 1969 through 1984, a period of high profile cases and changes to America's revered pastime. This placed Bowie under the national spotlight on numerous occasions. He consistently responded with grace and composure. He had a knack for proceeding in a patient, fair-minded, and professional manner.

Bowie grew up in Washington, D.C., attended a Navy training program at Franklin and Marshall College during World War II, and enrolled at Princeton following the war. After earning a degree in Economics, Bowie attended the University of Virginia School of Law where he was a member of the law review. Upon graduation, he joined Willkie, Farr, & Gallagher, the firm that represented the National League, and in this capacity, he came to understand the inner workings of major league baseball. At 42, he became the youngest ever to serve as Commissioner; at 6-foot-5, he was also the tallest. The combination of his stature, resonant voice, and professional demeanor made Bowie a commanding force throughout his 15 years in office.

In many ways, Bowie was the face of Major League Baseball. He proceeded with integrity, courage, and candor. When necessary, he confronted owners, players, and Hall of Famers, but always with conviction and class. In July 2001, approaching his 75th birthday, he appeared on an hour-long episode of EWTN's The Journey Home and described the important role his Catholic faith played throughout his life. Two months before that interview, we launched the Ave Maria Mutual Funds. Bowie played a key role in the founding, promoting, and growing of the Funds.

INTUITION, FAITH, & REASON

Despite my respect for Tom and Bowie, I was unsure about the marketability of a Catholic mutual fund. I told them I would give serious thought to the idea and get back to them with my decision about whether or not I wished to become involved.

My first step in undertaking that serious thought was to consult my most trusted and beloved advisor, Judi, my wife, best friend, and a person who sees things from a point of view that is distinct from my own. Her middle name is Pearl, and she has proven to be my "Pearl of Great Value" (Matthew 13:44) over more than 50 years of marriage. As in Jesus' parable about the man who sold everything he had in order to possess the one object whose value was beyond measure, Judi is my greatest treasure. She consistently presents an amazing blend of intuition, faith, and reason.

We met in high school and married soon after college. I was introduced to Judi by a mutual friend, Marcia (Walker) Byrnes, who told me, "You'll like Judi Arnold. She's the smartest girl at Immaculata High School, and also the best athlete." Marcia was right, and I shall be forever grateful to her. Marcia remained a close friend until her death from cancer in 2005.

Judi listened as I recounted my meeting with Tom and Bowie and described their idea. She pondered the notion of a Catholic mutual fund, and then, very logically and cogently, laid out a series of questions that were different from the things I had been thinking about:

- "What would be required of you in running such a fund?"

- "How would it transform your investment practice?"
- "What are the opportunities and risks involved?"

I didn't have answers to any of them. In fact, I realized that the answers probably wouldn't be obtainable for some time — not until after preparations for such a fund were well underway, in all likelihood. Judi's questions helped me to envision the scope of the task that Tom and Bowie wanted me to take on. I began to see that the implications for my professional life were extensive. Judi may have sensed some anxiety stirring within me (and the need for some countervailing reassurance).

"Well," she said, "you know Tom and Bowie. You know they're honest, they're good businessmen, and they're faithful Catholics."

And then she added playfully...

"Besides, they're both devoted to the Blessed Mother, so how bad could a mutual fund called 'Ave Maria' be?"

Judi provided the impetus I needed to really explore the idea. If her reaction had been negative, I probably would have gone no further. But I dove into some basic research.

In 2001 there were approximately 60 million Catholics in the U.S., of which roughly half were adults. At least six million of those were investors, and various studies of Church attendance suggested that 1.2 million could be considered regular Mass-goers active in their parishes, pro-life, and faithful to the Magisterium of the Church. This would be our primary target market, 1,200,000 Catholics. Of course, we would also strive to inspire as many other investors as possible, particularly people from all faith backgrounds (or none at all) who would welcome the Funds' pro-life disposition. Who knew how many such investors this might be?

Well, I thought, 1.2 million isn't a bad number to start with. I told Tom and Bowie I'd give it a try.

CHAPTER 2

THE HEART OF
THE MATTER

For where your treasure is, there also will your heart be.

MATTHEW 6:21

Cognitive dissonance exists if on the one hand we are pro-life, but on the other hand, we discover that our investments have been placed with companies that support Planned Parenthood or entities that produce or distribute pornography. Abortion and pornography gravely undermine the dignity of the human person. Fortunately, Ave Maria Mutual Funds provide a life affirming opportunity. More will be said about abortion and pornography in subsequent chapters. For now, let's explore how the Ave Maria Mutual Funds came to be.

GETTING STARTED

When Tom Monaghan and Bowie Kuhn invited me to explore the potential for creating a Catholic mutual fund that screened out companies with ties to abortion or pornography, the first question that would have to be answered was: Is a Catholic mutual fund legal? I turned to our Washington D.C. law firm, Sullivan and Worcester, whose investment specialists advised that such a device could pass muster with the Securities and Exchange Commission (SEC), as long as we made appropriate disclosure of the fund's religious character in the prospectus, specifying the purpose of the fund and what kinds of companies we planned to avoid in our stock-selection process. Basically, the attorneys told us the SEC would view our Catholic moral perspective in the way it viewed the screening criteria of "socially responsible" funds — as an idiosyncrasy.

Having confirmed that our fund idea was legal, the challenge we faced next was how to give the concept some materiality — in other words, how to make it seem like something more than just an interesting notion floating around in the imaginations of three reform-minded Catholics (which was really all it was at that point). The obvious way to make it credible was to entice some high-profile Catholic figures into lending their names to the project. We were extremely fortunate to find several prominent people who grasped our premise, understood its potential, and were willing to attach their own reputations to it in a very public way.

First to sign on was the famous scholar, ambassador, theologian, and author, Michael Novak. He was joined by Phyllis Schlafly, the pro-life/pro-family activist and founder of the conservative Eagle Forum, along with Thomas J. Sullivan, a retired executive of McGraw-Hill (and a shirt-tail relative of mine by marriage). Paul Roney, who had gone on to serve as executive director of Tom's Ave Maria Foundation after the sale of Domino's Pizza, was added, not only to strengthen the Ave Maria connection, but to lend his personal credibility as a CPA. Adam Cardinal Maida, at that time Archbishop of Detroit, agreed to serve as our Ecclesiastic Advisor. Then, through Bowie Kuhn's vast web of personal connections — and, frankly, much to my surprise — we were able to snag Larry Kudlow, former Wall Street economist and now White House National Economic Council Director. When we had approached him, I hadn't expected that such a visible figure would be willing to lend support to so new and unusual an enterprise. Tom and Bowie rounded out the panel with Bowie taking up duties as chairman of this Catholic Advisory Board.

Assembling this group of distinguished individuals gave us a foundation on which to begin building and promoting the fund. But it did something else, as well, which was to widen the focus of the screening process we would develop. With Cardinal Maida's advice, the advisory board recommended that we make contributions to Planned Parenthood a specific criterion for excluding a company's stock, as well as corporations engaged in embryonic stem cell research. The board also decided to exclude companies that produced or distributed pornography, as well as those that provided non-marital partner benefits to their employees (though that last criterion would raise questions which we would find ourselves having to address in the future).

This process of refining the definition of what we intended to offer investors helped to sharpen our ethical vision. The Board felt it made the fund a more comprehensive reflection of Catholic moral teaching, and solidified the concept of Morally Responsible Investing. To me, personally, it made the project real in a way it hadn't been before then. For the first time, I began to believe that Tom and Bowie's idea had genuine prospects.

Getting our application cleared by the SEC proved a challenge — and something of an education. I had expected that a Catholic mutual fund might be viewed with skepticism by government regulators accustomed to the values-neutral approach that dominates investment thinking on Wall Street. What I didn't expect to encounter was an apparent anti-Catholic bias. Making our application in late January 2001, we were told it would take about 45 days to get clearance. As things turned out, it took three months, and a look at the circumstances connected with that extra time is revealing.

The SEC staff member handling our application kept sending it back to us with what, in most cases, appeared to be nit-picking objections. Our lawyers repeatedly redrafted the document to make it acceptable, and on each resubmission still more changes were required. My first assumption was that we were dealing with an attitude that is unfortunately common among some government employees, a mind-set that combines boredom with self-importance. But the objections gradually began to assume a pattern that suggested there might be some personal distaste for a mutual fund with a Catholic flavor. I confronted the individual, and my suspicion was confirmed by a remark that was as ignorant as it was snide: "If you're going to have a Cardinal serving as your advisor, why not just get him to put his imprimatur on the fund?" That an imprimatur is only applied to books demonstrated the ignorance. The tone with which this remark was made accounted for the rest of my impression.

I was outraged. But my attorney offered the nearest thing to consolation I was likely to get under the circumstances, that well-worn bit of folk wisdom: "You can't fight City Hall."

Was all this delay just the inertia endemic to government bureaucracy, or was there actual anti-Catholic bias involved? Was Tom's connection with the fund a factor? Tom Monaghan has attracted much attention, and no small amount of criticism, for his support of certain candidates and political causes, generally of the conservative variety. Even though our dealings with the SEC took place during the administration of George W. Bush, a strong pro-lifer, we still ran up against the iron rule of government: "Administrations come and go; bureaucracy is forever."

My suspicions about bias aside, the processing of our application took a positively mystical turn. The Ave Maria Catholic Values Fund was finally approved on a beautiful spring day, May 1st — May Day — the day of Our Lady (the phrase, "Ave Maria," of course, is Latin for "Hail Mary"). It brought back memories of May crownings from my 1950s childhood as a pupil in Detroit's Precious Blood School. If I'd had any lingering uncertainties about whether the idea of a Catholic mutual fund was valid, they were all completely dispelled now. Clearly, the Lord was working in His own good time. My colleagues and I were ecstatic.

NO COMMISSIONS

From the outset, I determined that we would offer a no-load fund — which is to say, there would be no up-front commissions (customarily 3 to 5 percent) or back-end commissions or loads. This ran counter to advice I received from several brokerage houses that insisted they would be much more inclined to offer a new fund such as ours if they got commissions at the time their customers bought in. Load mutual funds have always gone against my grain. I feel strongly that every dollar an investor puts into a fund should go to buy shares of the fund — not 95 or 97 cents of that dollar, but all of it. The Schwartz Value Fund had always been a no-load fund, and the Ave Maria Catholic Values Fund would be, too.

Naturally, as with all mutual funds, there would have to be internal management fees paid to a registered investment adviser, in this case that being Schwartz Investment Counsel, Inc. — my company — for the research, analysis, stock screening, portfolio management, and administrative services that make up the professional investing process. But those fees, currently ranging from 40 to 100 basis points (a basis point representing 1/100th of 1 percent), are normal fund expenses, not any kind of toll investors must pay to participate. This, it has always seemed to me, is the only fair way to operate. The effort we put in as managers is what makes the fund succeed. That effort has value.

The actual organizing of the Ave Maria Catholic Values Fund fit well within our expertise. We had an existing fiduciary structure in the Schwartz Investment Trust, under whose umbrella the Ave Maria Catholic Values Fund was established. We also had a proven Value Investing template to follow in the Schwartz Value Fund, in operation since 1984. We integrated the new fund into arrangements already in place. Sullivan and Worcester, our law firm of long standing, became the fund's counsel-of-record. Deloitte and Touche became its auditors, U.S. Bank the fund custodian, and Ultimus Fund Solutions served as transfer agent, fund accounting agent, fund administrator, and later, distributor.

MARKETNG THE FUND

Without commissions to encourage broker sales, we knew that we would need to place additional emphasis on marketing. We decided to take the Ave Maria Catholic Values Fund directly to potential investors ourselves. We secured the services of a Boston-area advertising agency,

Clerestory Communications, and launched an aggressive campaign in
Catholic media, built around the simple, direct theme: "Smart Investing
and Catholic Values." The agency bought ads in such national Catholic
publications as Our Sunday Visitor, St. Anthony Messenger, and Catholic Digest, as well as on Catholic radio (in particular, the nationally
syndicated talk show, Kresta in the Afternoon) and in some of the larger
diocesan papers.

We also experimented with selected general and business publications, including Time, Newsweek, and Business Week, none of which
generated enough inquiries to justify their extremely high ad costs. On
the assumption that Catholics concerned about the moral implications
of their investments would likely also be conservative in their general
outlook, we tried National Review (which was quite effective), Weekly
Standard (which was a bust), and two Catholic journals, First Things
and New Oxford Review (both too small and specialized to be productive for us).

What may actually have been more effective than paid advertising,
however, was publicity. We received excellent exposure in a wide range
of general and business media. The idea of religiously-based investing
seemed to tickle the fancy of business writers. But I learned something
basic about the PR business through this experience — that public
relations consultants generally have a limited number of good media
contacts, and they tend to use them up quickly. We went through three
PR shops in that initial publicity effort. Each had success placing stories
with a limited number of outlets. Then, the well would dry up, and we
would find ourselves hustling to generate fresh interest beyond those
reporters with whom each agency was closely acquainted. Still, the

effort paid off, and we received a significant amount of ink.

One of the most compelling "hooks" we had to interest news people was Tom Monaghan's involvement in the fund. Tom's personal story (spending part of his childhood in an orphanage, starting Domino's Pizza on a shoestring) had made him a particular favorite of writers who specialize in business stories with a human-interest slant. The main value of the "Tom" angle was that it put the face of a high-profile business figure on the story of Morally Responsible Investing. We were covered by the Associated Press and the Dow Jones News Service, and got great exposure in business magazines and major papers around the country (overseas as well; one big hit was Die Velt, an important German newspaper).

I even became something of a minor celebrity myself, interviewed several times on radio and TV. This unaccustomed personal visibility got me invited to the White House to serve on the reception committee for Pope Benedict during his 2008 U.S. visit. When the invitation arrived, I imagined Judi and me in the Oval Office with the Pope and President George W. Bush. The first hint that my fantasies were slightly too elevated came after we submitted the information required for our security clearances. We received a follow-up email suggesting we show up at the White House gate at least three hours in advance of the program. When Judi and I arrived, we understood why. The reception committee consisted of 10,000 people, all of whom were standing in a line that ran for about a mile around the presidential mansion. We ended up far from the Pope and the President, but grateful for the invitation that would not have come but for the growing publicity around the Ave Maria Mutual Funds.

The Ave Maria Mutual Funds story was manna from heaven for clever headline writers who rolled out punchy lines like: "Religious Funds Help Investors Keep the Faith"; "In Mutual Funds We Trust"; "Seek and Ye Shall Find a Fund"; "Money Manager Makes a Hail Mary Play"; "Ave Maria Sings to Catholic Investors"; and other variations. I have no doubt that we provided many of these scribes with their best opportunity to explore religious phraseology since their Sunday school days. But nothing can top the headline that appeared in Mutual Fund News, quoting CNBC's Maria Bartiromo, who began an interview by identifying my associate, Gregg Watkins, as manager of the "Oye Vey Maria! Fund."

Well, we took all the exposure we could get. In all, between advertising and PR expenses, the roll-out cost my company more than a million dollars. But where it worked, it worked well. We became a modest but recognized presence on the business-news scene.

NETWORKING WITH BOWIE

While we were gaining all this exposure, I invested countless hours calling on prospective investors. Many of these visits were made in the company of Bowie Kuhn. Having been involved in numerous Catholic causes over the years, Bowie had contacts in dioceses, schools, charitable organizations, and religious institutes all over the country, plus a Rolodex crammed with personal and business acquaintances. His connections and his boundless enthusiasm for the Morally Responsible Investing concept opened many doors, especially among Church hierarchy. Several bishops and cardinals were close friends, and even those who weren't held him in high regard.

Bowie once made an appointment with a cardinal to personally pitch the Ave Maria Mutual Funds for the archdiocesan investment portfolio. On the day of the scheduled presentation, Bowie called me to say he couldn't make the appointment due to a family emergency. I changed my schedule, making my way lickety-split to the site of that planned meeting. The cardinal walked into the room expecting to see Bowie, but instead found only me. "Glad to see you, George," he said politely, though with obvious disappointment, "but you're not Bowie Kuhn." (I had met him once before, and I was surprised he remembered me.) When the cardinal heard about Bowie's emergency, he very graciously spent 45 minutes with me. His Eminence expressed great concern, showing his respect and admiration for Bowie, whom he had never met.

I began to sense Bowie's unique value to our project very early in the development phase. In 2001, I mentioned to some friends that Bowie Kuhn would be participating in a strategy session for this new mutual fund I was planning, and they asked if they might stop by and meet him. "Sure," I said, thinking nothing of it. The next thing I knew, I was getting calls from friends, clients, family members, professional colleagues — every manner of acquaintance — asking: "Can I drop by? Mind if I bring my wife and kids?" We finally had to arrange for a large meeting room at the Birmingham Athletic Club, about a mile from my office, and served coffee and doughnuts to a crowd of over 100 people. It proved to be an unexpected kick start for the Ave Maria Catholic Values Fund. One attendee wrote a check for $300,000 on the spot, becoming one of our earliest large shareholders.

Bowie's personal appeal also reached deeply into the realm of media.

I remember a particular occasion when I was to be interviewed by The Wall Street Journal. It was one of those loose, next-time-you're-in-town arrangements with a staff writer of decidedly junior status. The next time I was in town, I phoned to see if it would be convenient for her to do the interview, casually mentioning that Bowie Kuhn had made the trip to New York with me.

We set a meeting time, and when Bowie and I showed up, we found ourselves facing not only the young writer, but some of her male colleagues, plus an editor. They were eager to quiz Bowie about the current state of Major League Baseball, that season's prospects for the Yankees, and other sports-business topics. He regaled them with his repertoire of fascinating baseball tales, including the fabled saga of his 1974 clash with Yankees owner, George Steinbrenner. But along the way, the Ave Maria Mutual Funds got mentioned, and the result was some very nice publicity in the Wall Street Journal.

The Bowie charm was an asset in dealing with religious media as well. The World Over — Live, EWTN's public affairs program hosted by Raymond Arroyo (network news director), had long been at the top of my Catholic media hit list. Numerous calls to the show's producer always drew the same response: the interview schedule was full. I mentioned my frustration to Tom Monaghan, who suggested I offer Bowie for a joint interview. Bowie said he'd be happy to help, I called EWTN once more, and a week later, the two of us were in the network's studio in Birmingham, Alabama.

We got an entire hour of air time, the first half of which was devoted to Bowie, his baseball adventures, and his involvements in assorted Catholic good works. The second half focused on Morally Responsible

Investing, with Bowie doing most of the talking, even about the Ave Maria Mutual Funds. My function in the discussion was mainly to answer viewer call-in questions about investing. But we gained terrific exposure to the EWTN audience, about 2.3 million at the time. Arroyo even had our toll-free phone number (866-AVE MARIA) superimposed on the screen. It turned out to be one of the most productive media contacts we ever made.

While Bowie would have been the first to admit he wasn't an investment expert, he understood the basic principles of investing. More importantly, he understood and had a great sensitivity to people — all kinds of people. In fact, it was his direct influence that brought Larry Kudlow to our Catholic Advisory Board. I had approached Larry originally, and he declined, wishing us well in our endeavor, but insisting that he was serving on too many boards and committees already. I wasn't willing to give up, since I knew that having someone of Larry Kudlow's reputation and visibility on our board would give us the heft we needed. So I called Bowie Kuhn into action.

I made arrangements for us to see Larry at his office, and Bowie did his magic. He talked about our mission, the importance of the work we had undertaken, and how we were trying to offer Catholics an opportunity to invest in a manner consistent with their faith. Larry, a convert to Catholicism and strongly pro-life, identified with all that. Bowie proceeded to point out how our long-term goal was to change the culture by influencing corporate America to stop supporting abortion. I began to notice that Larry was listening to what Bowie was telling him with a level of absorption I had never elicited in my previous attempts to explain our project.

Bowie turned Larry around completely. He did it quietly and persuasively by making Larry see that helping us wouldn't be a burden, but rather an opportunity to advance an important moral initiative. It was a masterful stroke of salesmanship — and I mean salesmanship in the most positive and constructive sense. Bowie was a good salesman because he believed in his cause, and so was able to speak from the heart. Once more it had its effect; Larry Kudlow joined our board on the spot.

In addition to the circles of media, sports and Church, Bowie's contacts also extended deeply into the corporate world. He knew executives by the dozen — which proved extremely useful in cultivating relationships for many purposes. Bowie would phone CEOs of large corporations, asking that they accommodate my analysts with interviews and information as part of our investment research process. This was especially effective if the CEOs happened to be Catholic. But even if they weren't, Bowie Kuhn's name carried a lot of weight.

THE HEART OF THE MATTER

This book is about participating in the capital markets in a purposeful, reasoned and ethical way. The moral imperative of wise investment management demands that we conduct our financial lives with the understanding that in all we do, we stand under the watchful eye of God. For where our treasure is, so too is our heart. Throughout the journey of life, we are given opportunities to form a loving heart through daily decisions. Morally Responsible Investing helps investors remain focused on the heart of the matter.

Everyone wants to be happy and for people of faith, happiness comes from living a life of integrity. A consistent moral ethic, rooted in truth, is integral to who we are. The Ave Maria Mutual Funds provide a life affirming opportunity. The heart of the matter, from the perspective of the Ave Maria Mutual Funds, involves helping pro-life investors place their treasure where their heart is and to achieve good results over time.

By the end of that first year, the Ave Maria Catholic Values Fund had more than 3,000 shareholders. Now, 17 years later, the Ave Maria Mutual Funds have more than 100,000 shareholders spread across five different mutual funds. Later, I will discuss how my firm of highly educated, experienced, and talented investment professionals has helped these 100,000+ investors (mostly Catholics) do well by doing good for their pocket books, their souls, and the Catholic Church.

CHAPTER 3

A LIFETIME
PREPARING

You see, George, you really have a wonderful life.[1]
— CLARENCE

After getting over my perplexity at the idea proposed by Tom Monaghan and Bowie Kuhn of starting a Catholic mutual fund, it occurred to me that perhaps I had been preparing for this endeavor my entire life. I mean that in more than the professional sense, having started my career with the venerable Detroit investment house, William C. Roney & Company, whose principal was a devout Catholic of high moral convictions. There were signs in my teen years — even my early childhood — which might have suggested this turn my career would take.

THE GIFT OF CATHOLIC EDUCATION

Born into a family with strong entrepreneurial instincts, I spent my elementary years in Detroit's Precious Blood School, run by the Adrian Dominican Sisters. It amazes and saddens me to see how this order has changed. Nowadays, the Adrian Dominicans are very much taken up with feminism, peace studies, and nature spirituality, but "back in the day," they were known as super-strict disciplinarians. I recall a classmate, Ted Holloway, who considered Precious Blood more regimented than the private military school from which he had transferred. My own experience tended to confirm his impression.

Located in a largely blue-collar neighborhood in northwest Detroit, Precious Blood cost a family $20 a year for the first child attending; additional siblings were free. In the case of my own family, that meant my three brothers and I all attended at an average yearly tuition of $5.00, an unimaginable educational bargain today. But this was the 1950s, when parochial schools were staffed almost entirely by nuns, who worked for no pay, and the supply of habited teachers seemed virtually limitless.

Low cost and the Sisters' zeal for teaching the Faith in a straight-forward and dependable manner guaranteed full classrooms, which averaged 64 students and made discipline a top priority. Looking back, the quickness of a nun with her trusty ruler — that staple of so many Catholic jokes and reminiscences — makes complete sense. It was a matter of fending off utter chaos. But these Sisters accomplished much. They taught us the Golden Rule, made clear the difference between appropriate and inappropriate behavior, and impressed upon us the importance of trying to imitate Jesus and the Blessed Mother. The crucifix in every classroom provided a constant reminder that Christ died even for the sins of a bunch of rowdy, working-class kids.

It all had its effect, which became especially clear to me at our 50th class reunion, held September 13, 2008. Fifty-two members of the eighth-grade class of 1958 showed up, some coming from as far away as California, Florida, Texas, and Washington. It was inspiring to hear how many still practiced the Faith and had passed it on to their children and grandchildren. Soon, we will celebrate our 60th class reunion.

The power of Catholic education in the 1950s is evident to me now. My attitude at the time was something other than enthusiasm. I was terrified of the nuns, though fear never seemed to keep me from the rascally ways that regularly brought me under the wilting gaze of those formidable women. Somehow their lessons about the importance of doctrine, morals, and ambition seeped into my troublemaking, pre-adolescent brain — especially the importance of working hard and having ambition.

Catholic education, then as now, relies on the generosity of the families attending the school, the alumni, and the surrounding community. We held fundraisers throughout the year. By volunteering, I discovered a talent for salesmanship and a knack for fundraising. We sold raffle tickets, Christmas cards, and religious articles. My parents encouraged me to be creative, courteous, and diligent. They understood the benefits of perseverance and discipline, and the satisfaction of a job well done.

A Catholic education is one of the best investments one can make. It is a gift that enriches you throughout life and a gift that keeps on giving.

THE GIFT OF FAMILY

My folks were big on self-reliance, especially my mother, Marian Schwartz, who was a strong woman much focused on cultivating character in her five children: my three older brothers — Walter, Bill and Greg — me, and my little sister, Marianne.

Mom stressed that character showed in a crisis, but you had to work at developing it so you'd have it when it counted. "Always do what you say you're going to do," was one of her favorite pieces of advice. She maintained that too many people over-promise and underperform. Far better to under-promise and then perform beyond expectations.

It was a bit of wisdom which has stuck with me; its truth demonstrated again and again in my investment practice. If I project a return for my clients of 8 to 9 percent, a 10 percent return is greeted as a windfall. On the other hand, if I indicate that 12 percent is the goal, but only hit 10, the very same 10 percent that would otherwise make me a hero is viewed with disappointment.

My dad, Walter Schwartz, provided me with our family's practical perspective on the work-a-day world. He was a lifelong businessman and heir to the American immigrant story. His father, Paul, had arrived in America in 1909 (at age 19), after a condiment-making business he'd operated in Germany with his brother and father was somehow judged a critical national asset and taken over by the Kaiser's government. "Opa," as he would later be known to his grandchildren, was introduced to American free enterprise working in a German-language tavern, where his pay was $2.00 a week and as he said, "all the food I could steal." With classic immigrant pluck, Opa capitalized on his skill at making mustard and vinegar, building a new condiments business, which he eventually sold to the Great Atlantic & Pacific Tea Company (A&P), one of the pioneers of American supermarkets.

Opa never forgot the workman's skills that were the basis of his business success. He would brag to his grandchildren about how he could roll a wooden barrel filled with 300 pounds of mustard across the room, making it go anywhere he wanted, all with one finger. At the outbreak of World War I, he received a friendly greeting from the Kaiser, urging him to come home and defend the "Vaterland," to which he replied with the German equivalent of, "Yeah, right!"

My grandmother's story illustrates another aspect of the immigrant experience. She too had come to America as a teenager, but in the capacity of something rather like an indentured servant. Anna — or "Oma," as we called her — worked as an upstairs maid for a Jewish doctor in New Jersey. The memory of those days gave her a deep appreciation for hard, menial work and those who did it. She and Opa met at a German social club, and the rest is family history.

Steeped in that tradition of boot-strap initiative, my father made his mark in Detroit's machine tools industry. He always counseled me to "do something you like," observing that, "you'll probably be good at it, and you'll make a good living." While my youthful dreams inclined me to crave more than just a "good living," the wisdom of his advice has been borne out. I've been fortunate to spend my adult life doing work I enjoy, and I've made quite a nice living, learning something about self-reliance in the process: It's better to earn money than to win it, inherit it, or have it given to you. A thousand dollars gained through your own effort brings more genuine satisfaction than ten thousand you fall into.

Both of my parents were great education advocates, and when my days at Precious Blood were over, they sent me to another superb Catholic school, Detroit Catholic Central High School. Run by the Basilian Fathers, Catholic Central was known for the motto, "Teach me goodness, discipline, and knowledge."

The Basilians took that motto seriously — not only the words, but the order of priorities. Morality was first on their agenda, and they were no shrinking violets in promoting it. Discipline was the primary method of instruction, right up to corporal punishment. But their toughness was based in love. To this day, I remain in awe of these fine and dedicated men. It was my great privilege to serve on the Catholic Central High School Board of Directors for several years.

ON BEHALF OF LIFE

My parents were pro-life in the way most Catholics in the 1950s and early 1960s were pro-life — abortion as a right guaranteed by the Constitution would have been unthinkable to them. Likewise, they readily perceived the harmful effects of pornography and other sources of unwholesome influence. This was the common Christian understanding of the day, and it provided the fertile soil in which conscience could take root.

But it was the Basilian Fathers of Catholic Central who first opened my eyes to the specific evils of abortion. I think my teachers could see the moral revolution that was looming on the horizon. They made us face the horrors of a society willing to kill its babies — often taking flak from people who didn't want to think about such things — and it was their candor and courage that set me on the path toward my later-life emergence into the activism of Morally Responsible Investing.

With the advantage of perspective, I am even more impressed today as I reflect on the faculty who spoke the truth about abortion during my formative years in high school. I graduated from Catholic Central in 1962, eleven years before Roe v. Wade, the U.S. Supreme Court decision that legalized abortion. That 1973 decision denied Constitutional protection to the unborn, contending that consensus concerning when life begins did not exist. Of course, more than a decade before this infamous decision, my Catholic Central High School teachers demonstrated clearly that there was no doubt when life begins. We all understood the medical fact that life begins at conception. Surely the Supreme Court could have and should have ruled accordingly.

Tragically, more than 50 million unborn children in the United States have lost their lives due to the Supreme Court's refusal to stand by the truth of when life begins. Today, no credible person denies the medical fact that human life begins at conception. And yet, the killing continues — more than a million human beings every year in the United States.

Significantly, during the oral argument in Roe, even the attorney advocating for abortion conceded that if the Court were to find that the unborn human being is a person pursuant to the 14th Amendment (enacted following the Civil War to ensure equal protection for all), then the case for abortion collapses.

Roe is as deeply flawed as the Dred Scott decision that preceded it by a little over a hundred years. In both cases, the Supreme Court denied the truth that all human beings are persons protected by the Constitution. In one case, the right to life of an innocent human being; in the other, the right to human dignity as a person meriting all the rights and privileges of these United States.

I am forever indebted to the faculty of Catholic Central High School and their commitment to truth. I am particularly grateful for their instruction on the sanctity of life.

CULTIVATING CHARACTER

Neither my parents nor I ever considered any sort of education appropriate for me other than Catholic education — which continued through the Jesuit-founded University of Detroit. Not that a Jesuit school was without its quirks. By the mid-1960s, the Society of Jesus was well on its way to gaining its current baleful reputation as a leftist debating club.

I recall one professor (a layman, as it happened, but very much under Jesuit influence) who spent much time praising the virtues of labor unions. With my mother's help, I crafted an essay critiquing compulsory unionization, arguing how, in the name of protecting workers from the depredations of evil, profit-mongering companies, unions crippled imagination and stifled initiative. The instructor returned my paper with a note calling the essay "a great diatribe" and speculated that I must come from a family of "union busters." I will confess to a less-than-sympathetic attitude toward unionization which dates from an internship I had one summer during college at the Dodge Truck Assembly plant in Warren, Michigan.

The union members whom I worked with, side-by-side, resented a college kid working efficiently and complained that I was making them look bad. I dismissed their criticism until one incident provided me with an insight that has stuck with me all my life. A container had fallen off one of the forklifts driven by a union operator, strewing millions of tiny machine screws all over the floor and virtually shutting down a full day's production. I and several of my fellow interns were recruited to clean up the mess because the union operators refused to do anything other than drive their lifts. "Work rules," they insisted. Unions undoubtedly played their part in lifting workers from the depths of exploitation, but they long ago abandoned that noble role. There are ways to protect the rights of workers without crippling the industries on which their jobs depend.

Oh, and on that college paper, I received an A-minus. Considering the instructor's bias, that was both a compliment and a statement of his integrity as a teacher. Such was the atmosphere of learning created by the Jesuits, who even in their present state of confusion, are still recognized as champions of Catholic education.

CONSCIENCE AND COMMITMENT

The influence of my parents, the Adrian Dominicans, the Basilian Fathers, and even the Jesuits combined to shape me into a person for whom conscience and commitment have meaning and importance. My outlook was evident early, as one incident from my teen years illustrates. Driving on icy streets, I was rammed at an intersection by a driver who, it turned out, had a police record with numerous traffic violations (and worse). I was summoned to testify about the incident some seven months later. When I showed up at court on the appointed date, I was met by a startled prosecutor who told me there had been a plea agreement in the case.

"I didn't call you to reconfirm that you should be here," he said. "We always call the witnesses to tell them they're needed. Nobody ever shows up unless they're called."

I just shrugged. "Well, you sent me a summons," I explained. "I marked it on my calendar, and here I am. You didn't have to call me. It's my civic duty to be here."

He was quite stunned.

I hope it does not exceed the limits of modesty to say that I continue to live by this understanding of personal obligation. In fact, my annoyance with the practice of reminder calls — whether about pending medical appointments or having my cleaning picked up — makes me something of a pain to those who no doubt consider it a service of convenience. In my mind, people should simply do what they have set themselves to do.

Some years ago, a young man in my neighborhood discovered just how prickly I can be on that subject. I had paid the fellow in advance to put up a Christmas light display on my house — a job he abandoned in the middle, leaving its completion to me. When he called some weeks later to ask if he could earn another fee by removing the lights, he met with my disdain.

"You've got to be kidding," I said. "You didn't fulfill your commitment to put the lights up. Why should I pay you to take them down?"

He was outraged, believing that I was somehow cheating him.

"Young man," I said, "I'm going to teach you something that — if you listen carefully and live by it — will serve you the rest of your life. Do what you say you're going to do, regardless of what it costs you, regardless of how much pain and discomfort you must endure. You have shown a lack of character by not following through on your commitment. I suggest you work on developing that character. It will make you a happier and more prosperous person."

I have often wondered if he took my words to heart. And I guess I'll always have to wonder, because I won't hire him again.

I do know that living up to commitments has served me well

from the earliest days of working, which for me began with a Detroit
News paper route at age eight (actually half of my brother Gregory's
64-customer route — an unofficial arrangement, since paperboys were
required to be at least 12). I handled the job well for two years, until I
was 10. Then I got sick, and in what one might call an "unfriendly take-
over," my mother sold the route on me. With my duties as an altar boy
and crossing guard, along with playing in the school band, she worried
that I was overcommitted and becoming overstressed.

ENTERPRISE, THRIFT, & FAITH

My first encounter with the risks and rewards of entrepreneurship
came at nine years old, shoveling snow for a neighbor, Mr. Rosenbaum,
for $1.00. He was impressed with my work, and offered me a contract
to keep his driveway clear for the remainder of the winter. His proposal
was simple: "I'll give you $10 now, if you come back and shovel every
time it snows, no matter how much or how little snow we get."

The risk to me was extra work at no more pay. But the upside
possibility was intriguing. I calculated that we probably wouldn't get
ten more snowfalls that winter, so I was likely to at least make my $1.00
fee for each shoveling. And if the season proved especially mild, I could
come out markedly ahead. I took the deal and won — snow was light
that year. This was an important lesson about the moral rightness of
a fair exchange. Both Mr. Rosenbaum and I had taken a risk, but in
so doing, we each gained what we needed. He was guaranteed a clean
driveway and I made money.

My entrepreneurial appetite whetted, I launched a series of childhood ventures. I learned the importance of drawing attention to good

service by cutting the lawn of our highly visible corner home. My dad paid me $4.00, since our yard was larger than most on our block. I offered the same service to my neighbors — who could see how well manicured I kept our lawn, and whose own yards were smaller — for only $2.00, which they perceived as a bargain.

I was caddying at the Detroit Golf Club at age 11 (as with my Detroit News paper route, beginning under the usual minimum age of 12; I convinced the caddy master I could handle the job), earning $3.25 per round, plus tips. On a good day I could do the course twice. It's a testament to the contrast between the world of my childhood and the world of today that my mother urged me to hitchhike the four miles between the club and home in order to save the 20 cents a day it cost for the bus (which she referred to with the quaint, Brooklynesque expression, "carfare"). No parent would consider such a practice safe in our current moral climate.

At 17, I had a summer job in a local bottling factory, earning $1.77 per hour stacking cases of Hires Root Beer and Squirt. The next summer I drove a Pepperidge Farm bread truck, delivering to grocery stores around Detroit. That was followed by my summer at the Dodge Truck assembly plant — 90 days only; if I had worked a day longer, I would have been required to join the UAW.

Not only was I an industrious youth, I was thrifty — another habit acquired from my mother, who was one of the all-time great bargain hunters. My brothers and I liked to take in Saturday matinees at the Mercury Theater, which was located next to Precious Blood School (and where, in 1952, the entire student body made a pilgrimage to see "The Song of Bernadette"). We immersed ourselves in Superman movies and the grade-B horror films so fondly remembered from the 1950s, like "The Blob," "The Thing," and "War of the Worlds," along with assorted westerns starring such notables as Roy Rogers, Gene Autry, and Lash LaRue ("King of the Bullwhip"), even the occasional old chestnut featuring Tom Mix. I would start the day with a quarter set aside from lawn mowing, snow shoveling, or caddying, pay the 14 cents admission fee, lay out a nickel for a Coke and another nickel for popcorn, and emerge from an afternoon of cinematic fantasy with a penny left over — which I would then save. Our modern age of wall-to-wall media offers no entertainment value comparable to that. Frugality is an advantage in life. It retains great importance to me as my wife, children, and grandchildren can attest.

But in all, I think the dominant characteristic derived from these experiences of youth is my Catholicity. The quest for piety and Christian virtue (though not always their attainment) has been a reality to me since my altar boy days. How well I recall memorizing Latin prayers in order to give the appropriate responses during the old Tridentine liturgy (Monsignor Hermes had little patience with boys who forgot them or pronounced them wrong); getting up in darkness on cold Detroit mornings to serve at 6:00 a.m. Mass (my father would have to drive me there on time, God bless him); kneeling on the hard marble sanctuary steps, as if in personal penance, and reciting the Confiteor (Mea culpa, mea culpa, mea maxima culpa — "Through my fault, through my fault, through my most grievous fault").

CHALLENGES OF LIFE

The nuns and priests who taught me were demanding — in some

cases, perhaps, overly so — but my schooling gave me a foundation of faith and prepared me for some challenges that would prove pivotal. The first occurred at age 17, during a picnic the day after my senior prom. Despite my athletic deficiencies, I foolishly chose to play touch football with members of the varsity football team. I slipped on some gravel, came down sideways on my right leg, and snapped both bones (tibia and fibula) below the knee — double compound fractures, with chunks of bone actually coming out through the skin. I was laid up with my leg in a cast for nine months. It proved to be a remarkable time of growth, during which time my mother taught me much about the power of prayer.

Seven years later, I would be involved in the crash of a six-passenger Piper Cherokee, en route to northern Michigan with my father, my brother Greg, and Dad's friend Andy Farkas (a former Washington Redskins all-pro football player). We were to inspect some property which the pilot, a real estate agent, was representing, when we ran into a snow storm and lost visibility. Lacking a rating to fly on instruments, our pilot/salesman was unable to find the airport. We ran out of gas and went down in the north woods. As we lay in the rubble waiting for help, me with my back broken in five places, I realized the extent of my father's faith and courage. He kept repeating, "Hang in there, George. God loves us. He'll look after us." This from a man who was enduring two ankles severely mangled, one nearly severed.

I spent a year recuperating, encouraged by my mother's words — "Whatever doesn't kill you makes you stronger." I doubt she realized it, but my mother was paraphrasing Friedrich Nietzsche ("That which does not kill us makes us stronger"). The 19th Century German philosopher was a man of profoundly antireligious sentiments, and as such, he had little in common with my mother. Throughout my convalescence, I experienced the redemptive force of suffering and learned about what the body can endure, about patience, and about the true source of healing. In the process, I discovered strengths I might otherwise never have come to know, strengths which were, in the most literal sense, given to me, and which would prove to be my sustenance throughout numerous trials and setbacks in my business life.

INVESTING IN LIFE

My life has been spent in investments, a world that might seem a most unspiritual realm of professional concern. But then, what is it that I have been doing these past 50 years? My career has focused on the analysis of investment opportunities and on advising people as to whether those opportunities meet their financial goals. To put it another way, I have helped people secure their futures and protect themselves and their families against the vicissitudes of life. And that, it seems to me, is a Christian service.

My professional résumé is quite simple, but the experience it suggests is deep. I received my degree in finance from the University of Detroit in 1966. Between 1967 and 1974, I served as an investment research analyst with two New York Stock Exchange member firms in Detroit: William C. Roney & Company; and Manley, Bennett, McDonald & Co. I then became senior investment officer and chairman of the investment committee at the National Bank & Trust Company of Ann Arbor, Michigan. I founded my own firm, Schwartz Investment Counsel, Inc. in 1980, and launched the Schwartz Value Fund in 1984.

I am a Chartered Financial Analyst charterholder and a Chartered Investment Counselor, and an active member of several investment professional organizations.

It may come as little surprise that my favorite movie is It's a Wonderful Life. I happen to share the same first name as the lead character, George Bailey, played by Jimmy Stewart. It's a Wonderful Life endures because it is a story everyone can relate to. Life is quite often challenging, but we are called to give it our best effort. In the movie, George's guardian angel Clarence points out how different Bedford Falls would have been if George Bailey had not positively impacted so many. Morally Responsible Investing has been a big part of my life's work and I hope my efforts and this work will continue to benefit pro-life investors.

In any event, I cannot express how deeply grateful I am that my professional expertise has made it possible for me to advance a distinctly moral effort, and in a very real way, to help spread the Faith. While the moral picture of modern American society is at best "clouded," history demonstrates that our nation's founding principles serve most nobly during troubled times. These are the times when self-evident truths must be resolutely proclaimed with charity and good cheer.

All are created equal (hopefully soon to be honored from the moment of creation) and endowed with unalienable rights — including the right to life, liberty, and the pursuit of happiness. These principles coincide with Morally Responsible Investing. This gives me enormous hope that MRI will be a powerful, enduring force for good. I am truly honored to champion this cause.

NOTES

1   *It's A Wonderful Life*, The Original Screenplay, Frank Capra, Cluny Media, at 224 (2017)

CHAPTER 4

ABORTION

Abortion is different.
Abortion is the killing of the innocent on a massive scale.[1]

— CARL ANDERSON

Protecting life from the moment of conception is the essential pre-condition of all human concerns. If children are not born, there can be no other human concern. This is why Morally Responsible Investing has a zero tolerance policy for companies that support Planned Parenthood, the nation's number one provider of abortions.[2]

Abortion erodes the essence of *family* — the foundation of every civilization, cultural movement, and religion in human history. Protecting innocent human life from the moment of conception has always received special attention in the Judeo-Christian tradition, and particularly in the moral theology of the Catholic Church. To select any other point in life's continuum would be — *by definition* — arbitrary.

Human beings merit protection as a distinct person from the moment they exist. That moment occurs at conception. From that moment, a distinct human being with a unique genetic code exists. This is an objective, empirical, scientific, and medical fact. At the moment of conception, a new individual who never existed before comes into existence. That individual will never be repeated. This person's particular genetic code distinguishes him or her as a distinct and unique human being. The failure to honor and protect this human being necessarily involves an arbitrary decision to favor some human beings over others. Arbitrary is the antithesis of justice. Stated linguistically, arbitrary is the antonym for justice.

THE LAW

Currently, the law in the United States says that the mother has the right to determine whether this new human being may continue to live. And if the mother is under age 18, some states permit a third party such as a judge (i.e., judicial bypass), or the grandparents of the unborn (i.e., parental consent) to decide whether this new human being will continue to live.[3] Aren't we forgetting someone? Who is looking out for the new human being? The "judicial bypass" and "parental consent" mechanisms focus solely on the *under 18* mother. What about the *under 18* preborn? Law exists to insure *justice for all*. Where is the justice for the human being in the womb?

Abortion's disregard for the life of preborn human beings demonstrates how abortion distorts law and undermines legal reasoning. At best, the analysis is woefully incomplete. Justice requires decisions based on truth. *Verify* comes from the Latin *veritate* which means truth. Law schools train students to determine the truth of the matter by thinking comprehensively, considering all parties, and rigorously pursuing the evidence. Why do so many law students, law professors, and lawmakers spend so little time thinking through, discussing, or writing about the most profound civil rights violation of our time — the taking of the innocent life of the unborn on a massive scale?

The United States Supreme Court's decision to legalize abortion in 1973 through *Roe v. Wade* rests on a false premise — the Court contended that consensus does not exist concerning when life begins. Even if this accurately described the state of science and medicine in 1973 — though the evidence suggests otherwise — the advance of technology soon made clear that life begins at conception. Isn't it time to reconsider the Court's question concerning when life begins? What are the medical facts? More than 55 million human beings have been killed in the U.S. through abortion since 1973. Isn't it time to revisit *Roe's* foundational premise? Due process? Equal protection? Justice for all?

Law schools train students to "think like a lawyer." What does this mean? It primarily means that students participate in a rigorous three-year experience to prepare to serve as objective, clear thinking professionals capable of comprehensive analysis and dedicated to following the truth wherever it leads. Students study cases and controversies to learn how to spot issues, assess rights and privileges, create just laws, resolve controversies, and facilitate justice. Abortion is different. Rather than applying the full force of analytical reasoning developed through rigorous case study, the analysis in cases involving abortion largely ignores the rights of the unborn.

A human being in the womb is merely at a different stage; a younger age, but no less human. Unborn human beings are an entire class of people. A discreet, defenseless demographic. Why are they bereft of rights solely because of their stage in life? This is a devastating disconnect.

CONSEQUENCES

The failure to protect all human beings from the moment of *being* is an injustice with both apparent and subtle consequences. Abortion alters — indeed tragically taints — every aspect of culture. Abortion weakens marriage and family, fractures relationships, and erodes integrity. Abortion's web of deceit distorts law, coarsens politics, misdirects education, undermines medicine, and diminishes dialogue. The fundamental fabric of community suffers.

Conceptually, abortion contradicts noble principles such as "equal justice under law," "we hold these truths to be self-evident," "all are created equal," "endowed with unalienable rights," and "home of the free and the brave." Moreover, abortion flies in the face of the foundational principle of justice — protect the innocent. Tragically, abortion violates the commandment — *Thou shalt not kill* and substitutes cynicism for the *true, the good, and the beautiful.*

The reasoning behind abortion is upside down and backwards, and ultimately, clashes with creation and the Creator. How long will the United States profess to be "One Nation Under God" and print "In God We Trust" on our currency, while permitting the killing of approximately 2,500 human beings every day; more than a million every year?

St. Mother Teresa understood the true nature of abortion. She knew what was at stake and she articulated the implications. She exhorted with prayer and she presented the truth with love. As with all holy people, she urged repentance and renewal. Her heroic words speak volumes:[4]

> "By abortion the mother does not learn to love, but
> kills her own child to solve her problems. And, by

abortion, that father is told that he does not have to take any responsibility at all for the child he has brought into the world. The father is likely to put other women to the same trouble. So abortion leads to more abortion."

Abortion destroys peace:

"I feel that the greatest destroyer of peace today is abortion, because it is a war against the child, a direct killing of the innocent child, murder by the mother herself."

Abortion imposes profound poverty:

"Any country that accepts abortion is the poorest of the poor."

"It is a poverty to decide that a child must die so that you may live as you wish."

Abortion begets more violence:

"We must not be surprised when we hear of murders, of killings, of wars, of hatred. If a mother can kill her own child, what is left but for us to kill each other?"

"Many people are concerned with children of India,
with the children of Africa where quite a few die of
hunger, and so on. Many people are also concerned
about the violence in this great country of the United
States. These concerns are very good.

But often these same people are not concerned with
the millions being killed by the deliberate decision of
their own mothers. And this is the greatest destroyer of
peace today — abortion which brings people to such
blindness."

"And if we can accept that a mother can kill her own
child, how can we tell other people not to kill one
another?"

Abortion erodes integrity:

"If abortion is not wrong, nothing is wrong."

The recent explosion of sexual abuse scandals is an outgrowth of
decayed morals and "Slouching Towards Gomorrah" aggravated by
the widespread acceptance of abortion, with the attitude that people
can conveniently avoid the consequences of their actions. What can
be done? How might our decisions surrounding investments awaken
consciousness and restore protection for the unborn?

ABORTION AND SLAVERY

In January 1973, the United States Supreme Court in *Roe v. Wade* ruled that women have a constitutional right to abortion. The dissenting opinion and numerous legal scholars have described the decision's abuse of power and unfounded legal reasoning.

The case hinges on whether the unborn human being is a *person* protected under the 14th Amendment — the guarantee of equal protection and due process. To find a basis for abortion, the Supreme Court literally depersonalized the unborn. During oral argument, the Court through questions posed by Justice Stewart, stated that if the Court concludes that the unborn is a *person*, the case for abortion collapses. The attorney advocating for abortion conceded this point. The audio recording of the oral argument compellingly captures this stunning concession. And still, the Court did not side with the preborn human being. Instead, the Court pivoted, claiming that consensus did not exist on when life begins. Therefore, the Court would, in effect, table this essential question until some future time, presumably when advances in science and medicine provided a definitive answer. The Court then proceeded to deny personhood status to the unborn. When uncertainty exists concerning ultimate questions such as the beginning of life, sound judgment dictates erring on the side of life. Why did the Supreme Court go in the opposite direction in 1973?

As in *Dred Scott*, the Supreme Court got it wrong. The medical and scientific evidence readily available in 1973 made clear that life begins at conception. In 1970, three years before *Roe*, the official journal of the California Medical Association, *California Medicine*, noted:

the result has been a curious avoidance of the
scientific fact, which everyone really knows, that
human life begins at conception and is continuous
whether intra- or extra-uterine until death. The very
considerable semantic gymnastics which are required
to rationalize abortion as anything but taking a
human life would be ludicrous if they were not often
put forth under socially impeccable auspices. It is
suggested that this schizophrenic sort of subterfuge is
necessary because while a new ethic is being accepted
the old one has not yet been rejected.[5]

Tragically, in *Roe* (1973) the Court applied the 14th Amendment's
"equal protection" solely to the mother. Moreover, the Court relied upon
a "right to privacy," a concept created eight years earlier in a decision
that established a constitutional right to contraception.[6] This expression
— "right to privacy" — does not exist in the U.S. Constitution. The
Founding Fathers[7] did not want the Constitution to be amended unless
strong consensus existed. The Court could have directed the advocates
to pursue an amendment to the Constitution. Unfortunately, the Court
has "amended" the Constitution through judicial decisions.

Why has the Court not revisited the question of *when life begins*?
Instead, the Court has stated that abortion must continue because
Americans have come to rely upon abortion as a backup when contraception fails.[8] But this goes beyond the role of the Court. This is
not analysis rooted in evidence. It is an outcome-oriented, public policy
decision. What would the decision be if the Court revisited the central

issue concerning when life begins?

Our nation began with timeless truths articulated in the Declaration of Independence. The Constitution followed by providing, in effect, an operator's manual for good government. And yet, the Constitution included a fundamental flaw stemming from a compromise concerning human life. The original language of the Constitution counted slaves as less than a full human person. The linguistic gymnastics[9] that denies personhood to the unborn parallels this flawed thinking. As a compromise at the 1787 Constitutional Convention, the delegates adopted the false premise that some human beings are property and can be counted as a fraction of a person. Known as the Three-Fifths Compromise, the debate centered on questions of taxation and representation in the U.S. House. Population impacts both issues.

For purposes of representation in Congress, the southern states wanted to count slaves; however, they did not want to count slaves for purposes of taxation. The northern states argued that the southern states should not receive more seats in the House based upon human beings who were otherwise treated as property. And thus, the compromise — a provision counting slaves as 3/5ths of a person. This *depersonalization* continued for nearly 75 years. The 14th Amendment, enacted three years after the close of the Civil War, sought to remedy this foundational flaw by guaranteeing "equal protection" and "due process" for all. But what about the unborn? Why are unborn human beings currently not protected by the 14th Amendment?[10]

The Court in *Roe* sidestepped this question, contending that as of 1973, consensus did not exist on when life begins. Nearly a half century later, no one doubts that life begins at conception. The Court should proceed as described in the Catechism of the Catholic Church:

> Human life must be respected and protected
> absolutely from the moment of conception. From the
> first moment of his existence, a human being must be
> recognized as having the rights of a person — among
> which is the inviolable right of every innocent being
> to life.[11]

Unfortunately, the unborn continue to be discarded as property and conventional commentary is that if the Court overrules *Roe*, states will determine whether to continue abortion. But such a result would disregard the medical facts concerning life and misinterpret the 14th Amendment.

Planned Parenthood, a multibillion dollar Goliath, is the prime mover behind abortion world-wide. Planned Parenthood receives more than a half billion in tax dollars every year through Title X Medicaid funding administered through the federal, state, and local governments.[12] Planned Parenthood also receives hundreds of millions of dollars from donors and corporations.[13] While I admire Warren Buffett's exceptional mind and success concerning investing, I'm beyond saddened by his prodigious support for abortion. He gave over $40 million to Planned Parenthood in 2014 alone.[14]

Planned Parenthood generates annual revenues of $1.2 billion and does not pay taxes because it is treated by the government as a nonprofit. They describe their profits as "excess of revenue over expenses."[15] This contorted expression enables Planned Parenthood to retain its nonprofit status. Planned Parenthood has the money, but what about truth?

The truth is that abortion kills an innocent human being. The truth is that those who oppose abortion are truly pro-woman. The truth is that volunteer organizations help both the mother and the baby in her womb. Women's pro-life pregnancy resource centers outnumber abortion centers in the United States. As of 2013, there were approximately 2,500 to 3,500 pro-life centers in contrast to approximately 1,800 abortion centers.[16] The following three pro-life centers provide an illustration of this work.

ArborWoman,[17] located in Ann Arbor, MI, within walking distance of the University of Michigan, provides a 24-hour helpline, a free pregnancy test, assistance throughout pregnancy, alternatives to abortion, assistance after the child's birth, and counseling for all impacted by abortion. ArborWoman partners with Emmaus Health[18] to provide constructive, life affirming services.

Mother and Unborn Baby Care,[19] located in Southfield, MI, has been serving women and families since 1984. The organization helps mothers continue their pregnancies by providing practical, material support. Additionally, they refer women to a network of professionals including medical, housing, and adoption services. They also provide long-term assistance for homeless mothers who need shelter as they bring their unborn child to term. Through the years, hundreds of women and their children have been helped.

Obria Medical Clinics[20] have as their tagline, "Compassionate, Comprehensive Health Care." They operate 18 centers — ten in California, five in Iowa, two in Oklahoma, and one in Georgia. They provide services for all touched by abortion, or the prospect of an abortion.

They are fully-licensed community care centers. Hundreds of women and their families have found comfort, practical guidance, and a fresh perspective through an Obria Medical Clinic.

While ending abortion faces formidable obstacles,[21] so too did the abolition of slavery. Eventually, with heroic persistence, effective advocates, and ongoing prayer, the truth will prevail. St. Mother Teresa consistently and persistently urged America to choose life. She put it this way while visiting Washington, D.C. in 1981:

> "God has given your country so much. Do not be
> afraid of the child now. Do not turn your back to the
> little unborn child. Stand by that innocent one. My
> prayer for you and for your whole country is that we
> may realize the greatness of God's love for us and, with
> that love, protect the unborn child, the greatest gift of
> God for each of us and for the world."

Morally Responsible Investing agrees wholeheartedly with Mother Teresa's plea. By having a zero tolerance policy against investing in companies that support abortion, the Ave Maria Mutual Funds offer a tangible way to take a constructive step on behalf of justice for the unborn.

PERSPECTIVE

The sanctity of life is the basis of our human uniqueness. We are made in the image and likeness of God. We read in the Bible that God knew us before we were formed and that even if our mothers forget, God will not abandon us.

Try as they might to kick up dust around the topic, abortion advocates cannot obscure the reality that abortion is the taking of innocent human life. This is the brutal truth which simply cannot be avoided. Moreover, the legality of abortion pollutes the moral atmosphere of society in general. If it is permissible to slaughter the most helpless and innocent among us, then on what ethical basis can we prohibit any other harmful act?

The acceptance of abortion throws the credibility of law into question and dilutes the moral fiber of our entire culture. So if you seek to invest in a way that is morally responsible, the starting point has to be avoiding companies that participate in or provide support for abortion, as well as any mutual funds that have shares of complicit companies among their holdings.

NOTES

1   *Mother Teresa and the Transformation of Politics: Catholics Are Called to Create a Culture that Prioritizes and Protects the Most Innocent Among Us*, Knights of Columbus, Carl Anderson (2016)

2   Disentangling the Data on Planned Parenthood Affiliates' Abortion Services and Receipt of Taxpayer Funding, The Heritage Foundation, (2015) www.heritage.org/health-care-reform/report/disentangling-the-data-planned-parenthood-affiliates-abortion-services

3   *Indiana House Passes Pro-Life Bill for Parental Notification Before a Teen's Abortion*, www.lifenews.com/2017/12/26; *Why Pro-Life?* www.whyprolife.com/parental-consent-and-abortion/

4   Mother Teresa's 10 Most Compassionate Pro-Life Quotes, Life Defender Team (2016)

5   *California Medicine*, the official journal of the California Medical Association (Sept., 1970; Vol 113, No. 3); https://www.ewtn.com/library/PROLIFE/NEWETHIC.TXT.

6   *Why Pro-Life?* www.whyprolife.com/questions-of-law-2/

7   https://en.wikipedia.org/wiki/Founding_Fathers_of_the_United_States

8   *Planned Parenthood of Southeastern Pa. v. Casey*, 505 U.S. 833 (1992)

9   http://www.ignatiusinsight.com/features2009/wbrennan_interview_july09.asp; *Dehumanizing the Vulnerable: When Word Games Take Lives*, William Brennan, Ph.D., (Loyola University Press, 1995).

10 https://en.m.wikipedia.org/wiki/Three-Fifths_Compromise

11 CCC, 2270

12 https://rtl.org/RLMNews/09editions/AreMyTaxDollarsPayingForAbortion.htm

13 http://www.nationalrighttolifenews.org/news/2016/08/tax-forms-show-buffett-wealthy-elite-fund-planned-parenthoodworld-abortion-empire-with-hundreds-of-millions-of-dollars/#.Wm5KmWnwbIV

14 http://www.nationalrighttolifenews.org/news/2016/08/tax-forms-show-buffett-wealthy-elite-fund-planned-parenthoodworld-abortion-empire-with-hundreds-of-millions-of-dollars/#.Wm5KmWnwbIV

15 http://www.lifenews.com/2017/04/20/does-planned-parenthood-receive-taxpayer-funding-for-abortions-yes-heres-how/

16 https://en.wikipedia.org/wiki/Crisis_pregnancy_center; *History of Crisis Pregnancy Centers – Mother Jones* www.motherjones.com/files/cpchistory2.pdf

17 www.arborwoman.com

18 www.emmaushealth.org

19 www.maubc.org

20 www.obria.org

21 In addition to the financial backing for abortion providers, abortion proponents dominate the media, the entertainment industry, and education. Shaping the message has been a key strategy of the abortion movement from the beginning as noted in *Aborting America* by Dr. Bernard Nathanson originally published in 1979, just 6 years after *Roe*; A recent example is a 71 page report released in January 2018 by NARAL (National Association for the Repeal of Abortion Laws, and subsequent to *Roe*, National Abortion and Reproductive Rights Action League) entitled *The Insidious Power of the Anti-Choice Movement*. NARAL was founded by Betty Friedan and Bernard Nathanson. Dr. Nathanson later became one of the most eloquent pro-life advocates in history.

CHAPTER 5

PORNOGRAPHY

Civil authorities should prevent
the production and distribution of pornographic materials.[1]

THE CATECHISM OF THE CATHOLIC CHURCH

There was a time in the United States, not so long ago, when federal law banned pornography. Virtually everyone agreed that pornography fell far short of acceptable community standards. Few disputed pornography's corrosive impact. But with the dawn of mass media following WWII, community standards began to fade. Comedy, music, television, movies, books, advertising, and art pushed the limits of good taste. The shame associated with pornography gradually diminished. Hugh Hefner launched Playboy. Others opened "gentlemen's clubs" and collectively the porn peddlers promoted "adult entertainment."

As society opened the door to the world of pornography, discussions simmered around community standards and what might be acceptable. Advocates proposed distinctions such as soft-porn, hard core, and obscenity. Degrees of pornography? Isn't pornography always obscene? Aren't we merely justifying pornography? Doesn't the decision become a matter of respect for the dignity of the human person and whether to protect that dignity — both of the participants and the purchasers?

A series of United States Supreme Court cases from 1957 through

1973 wrestled with these questions. The opposing sides presented perspectives concerning whether the Constitution protects pornography. The test the Supreme Court relies upon to this day comes from a 1973 case, *Miller v. California*.

Pornography advocates contend that pornography is a form of speech protected by the First Amendment. They claim a constitutional right to produce and distribute pornography and argue that preventing these activities violates their right to free speech.

Those of us who oppose pornography contend that pornography is not protected speech because by definition, pornography exploits human beings. All involved are adversely impacted. Pornography lowers standards, coarsens culture, and undermines respect for the dignity of the human person.

Scholars generally agree that there are nine categories of speech not protected as free speech[2]:

OBSCENITY

CHILD PORNOGRAPHY

FIGHTING WORDS

DEFAMATION (WRITTEN AND SPOKEN)

SOLICITATIONS TO COMMIT CRIMES

PERJURY

BLACKMAIL

INCITEMENT TO IMMINENT LAWLESS ACTION

TRUE THREATS

To be banned under the current law, pornography must be considered obscene. Is this a form of linguistic gymnastics? Isn't pornography always obscene? The first synonym listed in the dictionary for obscene is "pornographic." Truth provides the basis for justice. What is the truth about pornography? Since the words *obscene* and *pornographic* are interchangeable as synonyms, shouldn't civil authorities follow the truth and wisdom of the Catholic Church and ban all pornography as obscene?[3]

Banning pornography establishes a line of decency. Once society crosses that line, logic, analysis, and well-intentioned tests are insufficient to restore decency. While we can't put the toothpaste back in the tube, we can begin again. Raise the standards. Restore decency. Recover the culture. America's animating and founding principles make possible a nation worthy of the title "home of the free and the brave." Authentic freedom rests upon laws rooted in respect for the dignity of the human person. Let's restore respect and build, sustain, and grow a culture of life and authentic love.

For the first 180 years in the history of the United States, pornography posed little danger to American culture. State and local authorities banned such material under public nuisance provisions. At the federal level, Congress passed the Comstock Act, named for Anthony Comstock, a man who dedicated his life to advancing community standards in support of marriage and the family and in opposition to pornography and abortion. Precisely 100 years following the passage of the Comstock Act, the United States Supreme Court ruled in favor of pornography (*Miller v. California*, 1973) and abortion (*Roe v. Wade*, 1973).

Over the course of the last four decades, pornography has flourished.[4] The free and widespread availability of pornography has accelerated due to technology. The internet and so-called smart phones have put pornography at the fingertips of the masses. Morally Responsible Investing offers a tangible step in the direction of raising awareness, influencing corporate behavior, and providing investors with an opportunity that does not support or promote pornography.

As our nation has done when faced with grave disorder in the past, we can acknowledge both the natural and supernatural causes of the disorder,[5] and then, take both practical and prayerful steps. Presidents Washington, Lincoln, Eisenhower, and Reagan provide prominent examples of leaders who acknowledged that "In God We Trust". They called for prayer and repentance and reminded us of our nation's founding principles. They urged a course correction rooted in virtue and truth, and they recognized that America has been and should continue to be a beacon of hope for the world.

SIGNS OF THE TIME

In 1957, the Supreme Court issued the first in a series of opinions that lowered the standards concerning pornography.[6] Within five years, it became apparent that the spread of pornography caused a loss of innocence. In 1962, an interfaith group of religious leaders formed Morality in Media, Inc. (now known as the National Center on Sexual Exploitation) upon discovering elementary school children with pornography in New York City.[7]

Ideas, actions, choices, standards, and court decisions have consequences. In 1960, the FDA approved the birth control pill. In 1965, the Supreme Court approved contraception. And in 1973, the Supreme Court approved abortion. Pornography objectifies, commodifies, and exploits the human person. What had been recognized as disgraceful became acceptable.

The Supreme Court teaches with great authority. Unfortunately, sometimes the Supreme Court gets it wrong. Prominent examples include *Dred Scott* approving slavery and *Plessy* approving segregation. These errors took decades to correct.

The Supreme Court's ambiguous and liberal treatment of pornography fueled pornography's rapid growth. Roughly thirty years after the Supreme Court's pronouncements on pornography and the "Sexual Revolution" of the 1960s, Judge Robert H. Bork published *Slouching Towards Gomorrah*, an incisive account of what happened to the United States. The commentary on the book's jacket provides a succinct summary:

> From the collapse of popular culture to the general
> weakening of intellect, from the role of the Supreme
> Court as an agent of modern liberalism to the
> trouble in religion, from the assault of radical
> feminism on American institutions and freedoms
> to the "killing for convenience" of abortion and
> euthanasia, Bork has brilliantly encapsulated a
> nation and a culture on the brink. He courageously
> sounds an alarm for all Americans.[8]

THE INDUSTRY

Most pornography comes out of privately held production firms, some associated with organized crime. Corporations such as Playboy Enterprises also play a role. A January 2, 2018, *Wall Street Journal* article reported that Playboy's magazine reached a circulation peak in the United States of 5.6 million in 1975. Today, Playboy prints under 500,000 copies per issue.[9]

Playboy's founder, Hugh Hefner, passed away in 2017 at the age of 91. Rizvi Traverse, a private equity firm with controlling interest, intends to expand and diversify the business:

> "We want to focus on what we call the 'World of
> Playboy' which is so much larger than a small, legacy
> print publication,"

Said Ben Kohn, a managing partner at Rizvi who took over as Playboy Enterprises' chief executive in May 2016.

> "We plan to spend 2018 transitioning it from a media
> business to a brand-management company." [10]

Playboy plans a line of liquor, clothing, a New York club, and a music festival in Shanghai, and will move the "Halloween" parties and other sordid events from the Playboy Mansion to nightclubs in Las Vegas.[11]

Pornography is widespread.[12] The case for the exclusion of Playboy from Morally Responsible Investing is obvious. What may not be as obvious is that the distribution of porn now largely resides in the hands of America's communications firms — cable and satellite television operators, internet service providers, and phone companies. Add to that the video rental chains, on-demand "adult" fare in hotel rooms, and some of the leading retailers, and you begin to grasp the scope of the pornography market. The internet provides another platform for the distribution of smut. Inexpensive and readily available digital recorders enable amateurs throughout the world to flood the internet. Digital technology is doing to porn what it did to the record companies and movie producers years ago.

PUBLIC HEALTH

Mental health professionals and family counselors are reporting dramatic increases in porn usage among men, women, and teenagers. States have introduced legislation to address the spread of pornography as a public health crisis.[13] What was sold as harmless turns out to be toxic and highly addictive:[14]

- 40 million Americans are regular visitors to porn sites
- 70% of men aged 18-24 visit porn sites in a typical month
- 67% of young men and 49% of young women say viewing porn is acceptable
- In the U.S., internet porn generates nearly $3 billion per year
- In the U.S., the porn industry generates $13 billion per year
- 2.5 billion emails per day are pornographic (8% of all emails)
- 25% of all internet searches are pornography related (68 million per day)
- 20% of men admit to watching porn online

at work

- 13% of women admit to watching porn
  online at work
- The most popular day for viewing porn is Sunday
- The average age when a child first sees porn
  online is 11

Teenagers have pioneered a whole new genre of prurient self-expression — "sexting" — the practice of photographing themselves in provocative poses and then sending the images via cell phones. This has led to teenagers being charged with distribution of child pornography. They face the prospect of being listed on sex-offender registries. With these cultural conditions, many people feel there is little they can do to reverse society's slide.

COMMUNITY STANDARDS

In 1916, Margaret Sanger opened the first clinic in the U.S. providing and promoting contraception and eventually established the organization that became Planned Parenthood. She dedicated the remaining 50 years of her life to advancing a phrase she coined — "birth control."

It is in this "defining deviance down" context that pornography flourished.[15] While Margaret Sanger systematically and comprehensively advanced her "sex education" and "birth control" agenda, forces beyond our borders sought to destroy the moral fabric that had made America the most prosperous nation in the history of the world.

COMMUNISM & PORNOGRAPHY

Planned Parenthood, pornography, and the pill played pivotal roles throughout the 20th century, but another force was (and still is) at play. We have known of this enemy's plans for more than a half a century. This enemy proudly proclaimed pornography as one of 45 strategies to undermine America. Significantly, this enemy is expert at running disinformation campaigns.

On January 10, 1963, U.S. Congressman Albert Sydney Herlong entered into the Congressional Record strategies set forth in "The Naked Communist," by Cleon Skousen.[16] Some of the tactics designed to destroy America include:

- Get control of the schools. Use them as transmission belts for socialism and current Communist propaganda. Soften the curriculum. Get control of teachers' associations. Put the party line in textbooks.
- Infiltrate the press
- Gain control of key positions in radio, TV, and motion pictures
- Continue discrediting American culture by degrading all forms of artistic expression
- Control art critics and directors of art museums "Our plan is to promote ugliness, repulsive, meaningless art."
- Eliminate all laws governing obscenity by calling them "censorship" and a violation of

free speech and free press

- Break down cultural standards of morality by
promoting pornography and obscenity in books,
magazines, motion pictures, radio, and TV

Communists intend to conquer America by implosion. Nikita Khrushchev, speaking to Western Ambassadors at the Polish embassy in Moscow on November 18, 1956, said, "We do not have to invade the United States, we will destroy you from within." Precisely 40 years later, in *Slouching Towards Gomorrah*, Judge Bork described this cultural crumbling:

> That is why there is currently a widespread sense that
> the distinctive virtues of American life, indeed the
> distinctive features of Western civilization, are in
> peril in ways not previously seen. This time the threat
> is not military...

> The enemy within is modern liberalism, a corrosive
> agent carrying a very different mood and agenda than
> that of classical or traditional liberalism...

> So long as it was tempered by opposing authorities
> and traditions, it was a splendid idea. It is the collapse
> of those tempering forces that has brought us to a
> triumphant modern liberalism with all the cultural
> and social degradation that follows in its wake...

> The defining characteristics of modern liberalism are
> radical egalitarianism (the equality of outcomes rather
> than of opportunities) and radical individualism (the
> drastic reduction of limits to personal gratification)[17]

Communism clashes with liberty, particularly religious liberty, because communism rejects God. Without the freedom to recognize God, citizens forfeit the ability to appeal to a higher standard. The state becomes the ultimate authority. The ruling class sets the standards. Under such circumstances, nihilism, coercion, and totalitarianism eventually prevail.

Nihilism came into existence through a Russian revolutionary party not that long ago. This is a modern phenomenon, but an age old issue. Nihilism is:

> The rejection of all religious and moral principles, often
> in the belief that life is meaningless.
> PHILOSOPHY – extreme skepticism maintaining that
> nothing in the world has a real existence.
> HISTORICAL – the doctrine of an extreme Russian
> revolutionary party c. 1900, which found nothing to
> approve of in the established social order.[18]

Nihilism and atheism are the dark towers of modern times. Communists celebrate when nations die through moral decay. Nations that put their trust in God appeal to a higher order. America needs a course correction, particularly in the area of pornography, abortion, and the dignity of the human person.

The Judeo-Christian tradition provides the foundation for Western civilization and strengthens democracy. Unlike communism, democracy aspires to build up, not tear down. Democracy holds to timeless truths, not disbelieving atheism; to a loving God, not a coldhearted void; to a purpose driven life, not a life of power, subjugation, and statism; to a moral life, not materialism anchored in secularism.

Communism rejects God and universal truth. Consequently, communism rejects America's founding principles such as "we hold these truths to be self-evident" and that "all are created equal" and "endowed by our Creator" with certain "unalienable rights." Respect for the dignity of the human person lacks meaning to a communist because in the mind of a communist, human beings lack inherent worth.

When Barack Obama became president in 2008, he appointed Van Jones, a self-described communist, to a top post in the White House.[19] Mr. Jones became a communist during a prison term in 1992 resulting from the Los Angeles riots. Following prison, he worked for ten years for STORM (Stand Together to Organize a Revolutionary Movement), a communist inspired organization. When this entity closed, he joined Apollo Alliance, a radical environmental group. Eventually he worked for the Center for American Progress under the leadership of John Podesta, former Chief of Staff for President Clinton, co-chair of President Obama's 2008 transition team, and advisor to Hillary Clinton's 2016 campaign for president. Van Jones served as "special assistant" to President Obama for "green jobs."

While running for president of the United States in 2008, candidate

Obama spoke in dramatic cadence, with key compelling words, but ultimately empty expressions such as "hope and change." What did he mean by this? And why was he so taken by communism and so inspired by Saul Alinsky? Alinsky was the author of *Rules for Radicals* and a self-described "community organizer". He was born in Chicago in 1909 and a friend of the Al Capone mob. David Horowitz published a booklet a year after the 2008 election of President Obama. In it he writes:

> To understand Obama's presidency, Americans need
> to know more about the man and the nature of his
> political ideas. In particular, they need to become
> familiar with a Chicago organizer named Saul Alinsky
> and the strategy of deception he devised to promote
> social change...

> Of no other occupant of the White House can it be
> said that he owed his understanding of the political
> process to a man and a philosophy so outside the
> American mainstream, or so explicitly dedicated to
> opposing it...

> [Saul Alinsky's] preferred self-description was 'rebel'
> and his entire life was devoted to organizing a
> revolution in America to destroy a system he regarded
> as oppressive and unjust...

> Although he was never formally a Communist and

did not share their tactical views on how to organize a
revolution, his attitude towards the Communists was
fraternal, and he saw them as political allies…

Alinsky understood that there was something flawed
in the Communist outlook. But, [like leftists], he
never really examined what those flaws might be. In
particular he never questioned the Marxist view of
society and human nature, or its goal of a utopian
future and never examined its connection to the epic
crimes that Marxists had committed. He never asked
himself whether the vision of a society which would be
socially equal was itself the source of the totalitarian
state…

For Alinsky, the revolutionary's purpose is to undermine
the system and then see what happens. The Alinsky
radical has a single principle — to take power from the
Haves and give it to the Have-nots. What this amounts
to in practice is a political nihilism — a destructive
assault on the established order in the name of the
"people" (who, in the fashion common to dictators, are
designated as such by the revolutionary elite). This is the
classic revolutionary formula in which the goal is power
for the political vanguard who get to feel good about
themselves in the process.[20]

President Obama's administration closed the National Obscenity Prosecution Task Force in 2009, his first year in office. The porn lobby celebrated Obama's re-election in 2012. Roger Young, a former FBI agent who worked to enforce obscenity laws for nearly 25 years, noted that the Obama administration's non-prosecution policy "has caused material depicting adults to saturate the internet and flood movie screens, television channels, and DVDs — setting the tone for our culture."[21] It seems as though the Obama Administration was trying to harm the culture, and by extension, damage the country.

Pornography has reached epidemic proportions. As a culture, pornography was unleashed during the tumultuous times of the 1960's. Per *Slouching Towards Gomorrah*:

> To understand our current plight and the direction in which we are moving, Bork believes we must look to the Sixties, a decade in which the moral integrity of our nation came under full-blown assault. We have never recovered from that attack because the radicals of the Sixties have taken over or heavily modified the cultural institutions they once sought to destroy.[22]

Former President Bill Clinton and his wife Hillary embody all that the '60s represent. Per *Slouching Towards Gomorrah*:

> The spirit of the Sixties revived in the Eighties and brought us at last to Bill and Hillary Clinton, the very personifications of the Sixties generation arrived at

early middle age with its ideological baggage intact.[23]

Here too, Saul Alinsky played a formative role. Three years before his death, he was interviewed by Hillary Rodham, during her final year as an undergrad at Wellesley, for her 92-page senior thesis on Alinsky's theories. She concludes by favorably comparing him to Rev. Dr. Martin Luther King and others:

> The title of Hillary's thesis was "There Is Only the Fight: An Analysis of the Alinsky Model." In this title she had focused on the single most important Alinsky contribution to the radical cause — his embrace of political nihilism. An SDS radical once wrote, "The issue is never the issue. The issue is always the revolution." In other words, the cause — whether inner city blacks or women — is never the real cause, but only an occasion to advance the real cause which is the accumulation of *power* to make the revolution. *That* was the all-consuming focus of Alinsky and his radicals.[24]

Like communism, porn poisons the human person and society. We were made for so much more. Per the *Catechism of the Catholic Church*:

> The human individual, made in the image of God; not some thing but some one, a unity of spirit and matter, soul and body, capable of knowledge, self-possession,

and freedom, who can enter into communion with
other persons — and with God. The human person
needs to live in society, which is a group of persons
bound together organically by a principle of unity that
goes beyond each one of them.[25]

Law strives to protect the health and welfare of society. Given the
harm caused by pornography, Congress should establish standards that
protect the common good without undermining freedom of expression.
It falls to the executive branch to enforce the standard and to the judicial
branch to assess whether the standard strikes the proper balance.

"Censorship" has a negative connotation, but properly implemented,
censorship provides boundaries designed to enable freedom to flourish.
Just laws and standards foster liberty and justice for all. Properly defined
and implemented, censorship safeguards freedom for all. Princeton's
Professor Robert George, one of the world's leading authorities on the
natural law and a member of our Catholic Advisory Board, reflecting
on *Slouching Towards Gomorrah* and the challenges posed by pornography and establishing boundaries through sensible censorship noted:

> In the area of censorship, for example, there are
> arguments having to do with whether efforts to
> ban pornographic material that really does deserve
> to be banned will lead to the banning of material
> — literature, art, movies — that actually does have
> important literary and artistic merit... The question of
> what the default position should be is itself a matter for

argument and prudential judgment. It requires us to consider what damage is being done, especially to our young people, in a culture in which pornography flows as freely and flourishes as it does in our society today.[26]

Pornography is a pervasive evil today. Sex-themed marketing, music, and chatter seem ever present. A course correction is needed.

Because Ave Maria Mutual Funds exists to provide investment opportunities that stays clear of pornography and abortion, it should come as no surprise that evil occasionally rears its ugly head in opposition. One such episode occurred a few years after the launch of the Ave Maria Mutual Funds. On June 12, 2006, Schwartz Investment Counsel, Inc.'s fund administrator, Ultimus Fund Solutions, LLC, received a letter addressed to me and threatening harm if I failed to purchase stock in a certain corporation. The letter included demonic references:

> You have until July 4 to get the price to $6.66. If you can accomplish it sooner all the better that way you will not have to worry about hearing from me again but it MUST be done by then NO EXCUSES. And don't even think about going to the authorities because as I said there are so many choices for me to be able to reach out and touch your life that it is not worth the risk. Remember it is better to reign in Hell, than to serve in Heaven. TIC TOC…

The sender signed the letter "The Bishop." Six months later, "The

Bishop" mailed two pipe bombs — one to Denver, the other to Kansas City. Three months later, law enforcement arrested a 42-year-old former postal worker named John Tomkins a/k/a "The Bishop."

While the receipt of this letter caused considerable stress, it did not reduce our resolve. More than a decade has passed, and I'm pleased to report that Mr. Tomkins resides in prison (until 2039) and the Ave Maria Mutual Funds are thriving. In the words of St. Paul, "where sin increased, grace overflowed all the more..."[27] We remain committed to providing an investment option free from the twin evils of our time — pornography and abortion.

The evidence of pornography's devastating impact abounds. Studies reveal painful and mounting losses from addiction,[28] crime,[29] and divorce.[30] Fortunately, a growing number of politicians are stepping forward. Since 2016, at least five states (Arkansas, Florida, South Dakota, Tennessee, and Utah) have passed resolutions declaring pornography to be a public health hazard.[31] Georgia and Virginia are considering similar measures, and options are being explored by countries as diverse as Canada, Israel, and New Zealand.[32]

Those who decry the banning of pornography as a violation of free speech are numb to the realities of pornography. Though they may seem to be beyond persuasion through facts, statistics, and reason, we must never give up. We must charitably urge them to ponder the true nature of freedom. Speaking to thousands in Baltimore, Pope Saint John Paul put it this way:

America has always wanted to be a land of the free.

Today, the challenge facing America is to find freedom's

fulfillment in the truth: the truth that is intrinsic to
human life created in God's image and likeness, the
truth that is written on the human heart, the truth
that can be known by reason and can therefore form
the basis of a profound and universal dialogue among
people about the direction they must give to their lives
and their activities...

Every generation of Americans needs to know that
freedom consists not in doing what we like, but in
having the right to do what we ought.[33]

Truth sustained by love enables societies to flourish. Straying from
truth leads to dis-*integrity* — the dissolving of culture; disintegration.
Authentic freedom serves the common good. Solutions include restoring integrity, fostering *integral human development*, and implementing
community standards rooted in authentic freedom characterized by
respect for life and the dignity of all.

Politicians supported by the porn industry downplay its systematic
exploitation of all involved — participants and consumers. And yet, no
degree of clever arguments and seemingly sophisticated calls for constitutional protection can change the plain meaning of words and images.

Returning to this chapter's opening quote offers a way forward:
"Civil authorities should prevent the production and distribution of
pornographic materials."[34] While it may seem that the multibillion
dollar pornography industry is beyond our control, avoiding the stock
of companies that produce or distribute porn is a step in the right

direction. Authorities must take the necessary additional steps, and by doing so, they will defend and uphold authentic freedom.

NOTES

1   CCC, 2354

2   http://www.newseuminstitute.org/about/faq/which-types-of-speech-are-not-protected-by-the-first-amendment/

3   https://en.wikipedia.org/wiki/United_States_obscenity_law

4   *Ashcroft v. Free Speech Coalition* (2002) pornography that appears to depict minors might be permissible.

5   www.catholicnewsagency.com/column/the-100-year-test-2454

6   https://en.wikipedia.org/wiki/Jacobellis_v._Ohio; https://en.wikipedia.org/wiki/Roth_v._United_States

7   https://en.m.wikipedia.org/wiki/National_Center_on_Sexual_Exploitation

8   *Slouching Towards Gomorrah: Modern Liberalism and American Decline*, Robert H. Bork (1996)

9   *Playboy May Turn Page, Drop Magazine: Post-Hefner focus shifts to licensing, lifestyle deals built around iconic brand*, Wall Street Journal, B6 (1/2/2018)

10 *Playboy May Turn Page, Drop Magazine: Post-Hefner focus shifts to licensing, lifestyle deals built around iconic brand*, Wall Street Journal, B6 (1/2/2018)

11 *Playboy May Turn Page, Drop Magazine: Post-Hefner focus shifts to licensing, lifestyle deals built around iconic brand*, Wall Street Journal, B6 (1/2/2018)

12 *Ashcroft v. Free Speech Coalition* (2002) pornography that appears to depict minors might be permissible.

13 www.google.com/amp/s/thingprogress.org/republicans-return-to-war-on-porn-5694cab4eb2b/amp/

14 Aggie Catholic Blog (St. Mary's Catholic Center at Texas A&M University); See also, www.covenanteyes.com

15 Daniel Patrick Moynihan, "Defining Deviancy Down," *The American Scholar*, Winter 1993, p. 17.

16 www.fdfny.org

17 *Slouching Towards Gomorrah: Modern Liberalism and American Decline*, Robert H. Bork, p. 4-5 (1996)

18 https://www.google.com/search?q=nihilism+definition

19 *Barack Obama's Rules For Revolution: The Alinsky Model*, David Horowitz, p. 1 (2009)

20 *Barack Obama's Rules For Revolution: The Alinsky Model*, David Horowitz, p. 2 - 6 (2009)

21 https://world.wng.org/2013/04/obama.administration_fails_obscenity_test

22 *Slouching Towards Gomorrah: Modern Liberalism and American Decline*, Robert H. Bork (1996)

23 *Slouching Towards Gomorrah: Modern Liberalism and American Decline*, Robert H. Bork. p. 2 (1996)

24 *Barack Obama's Rules For Revolution: The Alinsky Model*, David Horowitz, p. 8 - 9 (2009)

25 CCC, Glossary – Person, Human

26 https://www.firstthings.com/blogs/firstthoughts/2012/12/robert-bork-and-slouching-toward-gomorrah

27 Romans 5:20; www.usccb.org/bible/romans/romans5.htm

28 https://www.focusonthefamily.com/marriage/divorce-and-infidelity/pornography-and-virtual-infidelity/stages-of-porn-addiction

29 https://fightthenewdrug.org/the-disturbing-link-between-porn-and-sex-crimes/

30 http://www.sciencemag.org/news/2016/08/divorce-rates-double-when-people-start-watching-porn; https://verilymag.com/2017/07/causes-of-divorce-effects-of-watching-pornography

31 *Porn Deemed Public Health Crisis, Harmful in 5 States*, Baptist Press, April 24, 2017; *Florida's House of Representatives Just Declared Pornography a Health Risk*, Time, February 21, 2018.

32 *Porn Deemed Public Health Crisis, Harmful in 5 States*, Baptist Press, April 24, 2017.

33 https://w2.vatican.va/content/john-paul-ii/en/homilies/1995/documents/hf_jp-ii_hom_19951008_baltimore.html

34 CCC, 2354

CHAPTER 6

MORALLY
RESPONSIBLE
INVESTING

I have set before you life and death,
the blessing and the curse. Choose life… that you
and your descendants may live.

DEUTERONOMY 30:19

While Socially Responsible Investing addresses a broad spectrum of economic, political and environmental issues, Morally Responsible Investing focuses on making investment decisions that support the sanctity of life, marriage, and the family. The sanctity of life and the inviolability of marriage are the cornerstones of society. As the family goes, so goes the culture.

Formerly self-evident truths about human nature and human relationships have now become fighting words. To proclaim such truths as a principle for investing is to risk persecution. We live in a profoundly confused culture distorted primarily by music, movies, sex education, pornography, and the abortion industry.[1] Extramarital sexual activity ultimately leads to disillusionment. Reserving marital activity for marriage promotes authentic freedom, sound health, and enduring joy.

Abortion will forever divide our nation because it is both immoral and inimical to fundamental principles of justice. Innocent human life must be protected or the integrity of the culture, society, legal system, and nation will disintegrate (i.e., dissolve integrity). Every election reveals this disintegration. The election and later re-election of Barack Obama as President of the United States with the support of the majority of Catholics is a profound disconnect.

Catholics make up the largest religious group in the nation, approximately 25% of the population. Without the support of Catholics, Obama likely would not have been elected President of the United States. A few days after the November 2008 election results, Cardinal George, the then President of the United States Conference of Catholic Bishops, published a statement on behalf of life:

> Abortion kills not only unborn children; it destroys
> constitutional order and the common good, which is
> assured only when the life of every human being is
> legally protected.[2]

Regrettably, the statement had no apparent effect on President-elect Obama. He became the most pro-abortion president in the history of the United States. He directed over one-half billion dollars a year to Planned Parenthood; four billion over eight years. He appointed pro-abortion judges. He led the charge to enact the Affordable Care Act (i.e., Obamacare) mandating contraceptive and abortifacient coverage. The Little Sisters of the Poor, EWTN, Priests for Life, and other faithful Catholic organizations opposed the mandate through litigation.

The battle proceeded for years through the federal courts and ultimately arrived before the U.S. Supreme Court. President Obama did all of these things in his first term of office, and yet, he was re-elected in 2012, winning the Catholic vote yet again. Catholic Bishops spoke out during the 2012 election, but according to Robert Jones, chief executive of the Public Religion Research Institute, they had little impact.[3]

What might have been accomplished if the four billion dollars President Obama's administration directed to Planned Parenthood had been directed to life affirming initiatives? Or infrastructure? Bridges, roads, schools... anything but to take the life of unborn children through abortion?

Every election cycle since 1973 has been influenced by abortion. When disorder takes root, reason and truth face an uphill climb. The logical consequences associated with evil tend to be subsumed by the culture. Once a society accepts the taking of innocent life, it is logical that a parade of horribles will follow: partial birth abortion, the selling of body parts, and the disposal of human beings as medical waste.

By restoring protection for the innocent, we will experience a new springtime. If we fail to do so, we will continue to see the decline and coarsening of our culture. The disregard for innocent human beings in the womb is the foundational human rights issue.

Morally Responsible Investing can only be morally responsible by having zero tolerance for abortion and total love for innocent unborn human beings, their mothers, and all impacted by abortion. It is time to provide equal protection for all. Indeed, it is time to restore constitutional order, reject abortion, and *choose life.*

A LESSON IN ECONOMICS

When my friend and Catholic Advisory Board member Michael Novak died on February 17, 2017, the thinking world lost a giant. He was a liberal early in his life, having written speeches for Mondale, McGovern and others, but became a Republican and a conservative as he matured. He was a renaissance man — an ambassador and a gifted professor of philosophy, religious studies, social ethics, and economics. Michael was also a defender of freedom and a prolific author. He will long be remembered for his groundbreaking 1982 book, *The Spirit of Democratic Capitalism*:

> Most religious thinkers lack a basic understanding
> of the economic life of man. Few theologians or
> religious leaders understand economics, industry,
> manufacturing, trade, and finance. Many seem
> trapped in pre-capitalist mode of thought...
> many swiftly reduce all morality to the morality
> of distribution. They demand jobs without
> comprehending how jobs are created. They demand
> the distribution of the world's goods without insight
> into how the store of the world's goods may be
> expanded... they claim to be leaders without having
> mastered the techniques of human progress.[4]

In a world where far too many live in poverty, finding sustainable and long-term solutions is imperative. Unfortunately, well intentioned theologians too often miss the mark as Novak states above. Three documents from the past two centuries provide a context for understanding insights from the Catholic intellectual tradition concerning the economy.

Issued in 1891, Pope Leo XIII's encyclical, *Of Revolutionary Change (Rerum Novarum)*, discusses a range of considerations including capital, labor, private property, and the need for fair wages and safe working conditions. This encyclical appeared at a time when the ideas of Karl Marx and other socialists began to take hold. Socialists contend that individuals should not own land, money, or industry; that instead, these should be owned collectively for the good of all.[5] History shows that socialism is fundamentally flawed because it takes away the incentive to achieve. Pope Leo understood that private ownership advances excellence, inspires inventiveness, and encourages sustainability and good stewardship. Pope Leo also respected investing as a means of wise and prudent planning.[6] Moreover, he insisted that the needs of the poor must be systematically addressed for the economic order to be considered Christian, and that the earth's resources are to be managed in a manner that serves "the common interests of all."[7]

In 1931, through the encyclical *In the 40th Year (Quadragesimo Anno)*, honoring the 40th anniversary of *Rerum Novarum*, Pope Pius XI emphasized the vital connection between economics and morality. Citing the unique human capacity to reason, Pius insisted on moral discernment in temporal affairs.[8] He cautioned against would-be stock manipulators and conditions that give rise to wild commodity speculations that undermine prudent analysis and forecasts.[9]

In 1991, to honor the 100th anniversary of *Rerum Novarum*, Pope Saint John Paul issued *Hundredth Year (Centesimus Annus)*, a sweeping commentary on economics, human liberty, and the conditions of life in a world that had just witnessed the crumbling of the Berlin Wall, an accomplishment in which Pope Saint John Paul and President Ronald Reagan played key roles. While noting communism's inherent flaws, Pope Saint John Paul cautioned capitalists to avoid communism's rejection of objective truth. He noted that when a market system:

> denies an autonomous existence and value to morality,
> law, culture and religion, it agrees with Marxism, in
> the sense that it totally reduces man to the sphere of
> economics and the satisfaction of material needs.[10]

These excerpts from the writings of three Popes over the past century briefly illustrate the contribution to economics and investing that Catholic moral philosophy offers. The Catholic Church, inspired by Christ and dedicated to faith and reason, teaches about the nature of man and the human experience. This expertise contributes mightily to morality in the marketplace and the world at large.

MARKET ECONOMY

Morally Responsible Investing embraces unchanging truths, and thus, has universal application. As such, Morally Responsible Investing applies and extends beyond the United States. A recent election in Chile serves as a case in point.

A December 18, 2017, *Wall Street Journal* article entitled "An Election Watershed in Chile" described Chile's presidential race as the most significant in the past thirty years because the candidates presented diametrically opposing views on the economy. The positions mirrored those staked out in U.S. presidential cycles over the past 10 years. The center-right candidate emphasized economic growth, market fundamentals, and individual liberty. The leftist, socialist candidate emphasized social justice, wealth redistribution, and government intervention.

Chile's economy suffered under the leadership of Socialist Party President Michelle Bachelet (2006–2010 and 2014–2018). An admirer of Fidel Castro, Bachelet emphasized themes familiar to Americans during the Obama presidency (and proposed to be expanded by candidates Hillary Clinton and Bernie Sanders during the 2016 election cycle): raising taxes, growing government, and increasing government spending. Significantly, the population that Chile's socialist leaders claimed to be helping knew better. The editorial put it this way:

> It's no coincidence that growth, productivity and
> employment slumped as the government raised taxes,
> increased spending, and passed a labor reform that
> places a heavy burden on hiring. The World Bank's
> ease-of-doing-business survey ranked Chile 37th in
> the world in 2013. This year it came in at 57.th [11]

Mr. Alejandro Guillier, the Socialist Party's replacement for Ms. Bachelet, promised to continue Bachelet-nomics; to substantially increase the role of government in pensions, and to push for a rewrite of the 1980 constitution. Low-income Chileans fared the worst under Ms. Bachelet's leadership. Mr. Guillier lost nine of the country's ten poorest districts, and ultimately lost the election to Mr. Sebastian Pinera.[12]

Though the failure of socialism in South America is well-known (and most recently on display with catastrophic consequences in Venezuela), the power of the media can blur the economic reality. Too often truth succumbs to the "dictatorship of relativism."[13] Social media's massive messaging capacity can shade the message. It is hoped that Mr. Pinera will stand up for morality in the marketplace:

> Yet Mr. Pinera has a history of unwillingness to
> defend the morality of the market economy. This is
> why the middle class is drifting left. Now that he
> has another chance, Chileans have to hope he has
> learned his lesson.[14]

Mr. Pinera ran as a candidate who could reinvigorate the economy. He is a billionaire businessman who understands the strategic importance of private ownership.

PRIVATE PROPERTY

Economic development depends upon protecting and advancing private property rights. Morally Responsible Investing supports, encourages, and facilitates private property rights in general and private ownership in particular. Investing involves private ownership.

A January 26, 2018, *Wall Street Journal* article provides new evidence concerning the essential link between private property, economic development, and sustainable development. The article describes technology that hopefully soon will enable the worldwide recording of property deeds. This would be a stunning achievement with wonderful potential. The software would make private property ownership achievable, and by so doing, reinforce the time-tested reality that private ownership raises everyone's standard of living:

> For a long time, Western economists failed to
> appreciate the relationship between private property
> rights and economic development. Karl Marx saw
> private property as the source of wealth and called for
> its elimination to promote equality. A century and a
> half later, we know that a country without a formal
> system for registering property rights limits its own
> economic development and prevents it citizens from
> realizing their full potential. It's a simple yet startling
> fact: The road to economic development runs through
> the county clerk's office at the local courthouse.[15]

How does the recording of private property ownership lift people out of poverty? Here are the latest numbers:

> The great economic divide in the world today is
> between the 2.5 billion people who can register
> property rights and the five billion who are
> impoverished, in part because they can't. Consider
> what happens without a formal system of property
> rights: values are reduced for privately owned assets;
> wages are devalued for workers using these assets;
> owners are denied the ability to use their assets as
> collateral to obtain credit or as a credential to claim

public services; and society loses the benefits that
accrue when assets are employed for their highest and
best purpose.[16]

When thinking about raising the standard of living, focusing on
the fundamentals is a good place to start. Just as Morally Responsible
Investing focuses on the highest human right (the right to life), and the
most fundamental principle of justice (protecting the innocent), third
world development would do well to focus on infrastructure rather than
polemics such as requiring underdeveloped nations to accept western
attitudes on sexual morality.[17] Providing an efficient system for recording property rights is an illustration of a fundamental infrastructure that
will yield a tremendous return. With the availability of satellite photos,
the Global Positioning System, and emerging software to collect, organize, and retrieve data, the world may soon standardize the recording of
private property on a worldwide basis. The software technology under
development is called Blockchain:

> Blockchain is an especially promising technology
> because of its record-keeping capacity, its ability
> to provide access to millions of users, and the
> fact that it can be constantly updated as property
> ownership changes hands. If Blockchain technology
> can empower public and private efforts to register
> property rights on a single computer platform, we can
> share the blessings of private-property registration
> with the whole world. Instead of destroying private

property to promote a Marxist equality in poverty,
perhaps we can bring property rights to all mankind.
Where property rights are ensured, so are the
prosperity, freedom and ownership of wealth that
brings real stability and peace.[18]

Private property ownership is the surest path to ending poverty. Facilitating private ownership worldwide would equip millions with the ability to manage, improve, and steward private property. This is authentic sustainable development. It is human nature to take pride in ownership. Consistent with the natural law, ownership inspires and motivates attentive stewardship, and by so doing, lifts people out of poverty, builds self-esteem, and provides a path to the future. A path energized by hope, dreams, and creative imagination. Human ingenuity is the greatest human resource.

GOSPEL VALUES

Life is a gift from God who sent his son so that we might have life and have it to the fullest. Jesus literally means *God saves*. One way we experience this saving light, this abundant life, is by virtuously utilizing our gifts. How will we use our gifts and talents? How will we invest our gifts and talents? How might we be both faithful and successful through our investments? And when successful, how should we use the financial fruits of our success? How can we live out our responsibilities to our family and community consistent with Gospel values?

The Bible's financial references have provided the basis for centuries of reflection. Some passages emphasize investing for the sake of providing for one's future:

> "The good leave an inheritance to their children's
> children."[19]

> "Whoever does not provide for relatives and especially
> family members has denied the faith and is worse than
> an unbeliever."[20]

Scripture offers no record of Jesus advising his disciples to "buy low, and sell high," but I believe that moral discernment enriches investing judgment. Companies which appreciate in value and whose shares rise correspondingly in price share common elements. They tend to be well-managed and have decision makers who follow sensible business practices, offer good products, and deal ethically and reliably with their suppliers, employees and customers.

If "like knows like" — and I believe this is arguably true — then moral people are better able to discern virtuous qualities that are not always casually apparent. Similarly, people of genuine and abiding faith tend to live out their beliefs daily, practice regular devotions, and conduct their lives with a degree of honorable self-discipline. This mode of living (which shows a certain parallel with the well-run company) disposes someone to the patient attentiveness required for successful investment results over the long term. It also reflects an internalization of the idea of "stewardship," a recurring theme in the teachings of Christ. Someone who strives to be a faithful steward of family resources (or the resources of others) will be attuned to practical prospects and responsible choices, and naturally averse to flashy get-rich-quick schemes.

Good business management may not necessarily be a direct product of morally responsible investing, but it does correlate with ethical awareness, a decisively moral concept. Moreover, the values at the core of a company's operational approach — that particular set of objectives, priorities and working assumptions to which key decision makers must give assent — will ultimately find expression in the firm's public image. How often have you heard that XYZ Corp. doesn't care about its customers or that it treats its employees like dirt? A company's reputation has a definite influence on investor attitudes toward any given stock.

Additionally, there is a growing trend to apply ethical criteria to what companies are in the business of *doing*. When considering the purchase of a particular stock, they will ask more fundamental questions, such as: "Do I believe this company's products or services are *proper*? Is the business acceptable to me, personally, as a *legitimate* endeavor? Are its practices and procedures *right*?" This kind of inquiry lifts investment decision making to a different level of concern, because it involves the element of *conscience*. This is entirely appropriate because when you acquire the stock of a corporation, you become one of the company's owners.

The reality of ownership is vividly illustrated when shareholders organize to complain that chronic poor performance by company management has caused the stock price to fall. The concept of the *proxy contest* is based on the fact that shareholders are owners with the right to express their views about company policies and procedures. The company you own acts in your name, not only in delivering value as an investment by maintaining and improving its profitability, but in what it does on a daily basis. The one and only fiduciary responsibility which a board of directors has is to the investors who own the firm. As an owner, you have the legal right to act if directors fail in their duty to represent your interest. Also, your status as an owner gives you certain ethical obligations with regards to the policies and procedures by which the company operates.

SOCIALLY RESPONSIBLE INVESTING

Today there is a heightened awareness about the role played by personal investing in the free enterprise system. It has grown over recent decades, encouraged by such factors as the collapse of communism; the fundamental flaws of socialism such as its disdain for private property rights (socialism shares much in common with communism);[21] the proliferation of mutual funds; the number of retirement plans in the financial markets; and investor involvement made possible by online trading.

This stockholder awareness has coincided with the growth of numerous socially conscious movements, both domestic and international, which have sought to influence the business community in support of — or in opposition to — a variety of causes. The end of the apartheid regime in South Africa came about largely because stockholders of major corporations and investors in important mutual funds were able to bring pressure on companies to *divest* themselves of their South African business holdings or to cut ties with other firms doing business in South Africa.

Likewise, motivated investors have played a significant role in putting race- and gender-equity issues on boardroom agendas, not to mention the environmentalist stockholder agitation that has assisted in prodding virtually all major U.S. corporations to "go green" (if, in some cases, more in their public relations pronouncements than in their actual operations). Indeed, company directors have come to expect pressure over policies and procedures, often related to issues that are quite peripheral to a firm's actual business. Annual meeting planners now take it pretty much as a given that some stockholder group will insist on floor time to promote one cause or another.

The rise of organized stockholder activism has been paralleled by the creation of financial products that enable individuals to express their social and political commitments through their stock purchases. A plentiful assortment of ideologically driven mutual funds has appeared on the scene under the label, "Socially Responsible Investing". The investment holdings of most such funds generally reflect judgments colored by social and political perspectives that would be termed "liberal" or "progressive."

Socially Responsible Investing tends to favor companies whose policies address issues that are prominent with the mainstream media, the entertainment industry, most college and university campuses, and the major not-for-profit organizations. Accordingly, Socially Responsible Investing tends to screen out corporations that allegedly "despoil the environment," "exploit oppressed minorities," "impede sustainable 'Third World' development," "contribute to international conflict," or create other situations of injustice (real or perceived). Consistent with the left's worldview, Socially Responsible Investing would not screen out companies that support abortion, pornography, or embryonic stem cell research as we do in managing the Ave Maria Mutual Funds.

THE BOTTOM LINE

The amount of money you invest influences a company's current stock price and impacts future price movements. It becomes part of the company's enterprise value, helping to determine its financial viability, the level at which it can function, and its ability to raise future capital. The stocks you hold are not just claim checks on some possible future reward (like lottery tickets). They represent ownership in real businesses that produce real products or services and provide jobs for real people. Your investment portfolio is thus part of the economic life of the nation. It has power — power which is in your hands — and power is a distinctly moral concept and time-honored concept. "I have set before you life and death, the blessing and the curse. Choose life..."

NOTES

1   *unPlanned: The True Story of a Former Planned Parenthood Leader's Courageous Choice in Favor of Life*, Abby Johnson, (2014). Abby describes Planned Parenthood's instructions to clinic directors to increase the number of abortions performed per month to increase revenue. www.unplannedthebook.com

2   Statement of the President of the United States Conference of Catholic Bishops, Cardinal George, (Nov. 12, 2008)

3   www.reuters.com/article/us-usa-campaign-religion/most-catholics-vote-for-obama-but-latinos-and-whites-divided (Nov. 8, 2012)

4   *The Spirit of Democratic Capitalism*, Robert Novak (1982)

5   www.culture-war.info/Socialism.html

6   *Rerum Novarum*, Paragraph 7.

7   *Rerum Novarum*, Paragraph 8.

8   *Quadragesimo Anno*, Paragraph 42

9   *Quadragesimo Anno*, Paragraph 132.

10 *Centesimus Annas*, Section 19.

11 *An Election Watershed in Chile*, The Wall Street Journal, Dec. 16, 2017, A15

12 *An Election Watershed in Chile*, The Wall Street Journal, Dec. 16, 2017, A15

13 Homily of Joseph Cardinal Ratzinger, Dean of the College of Cardinals, Mass for the Election of the Supreme Pontiff, St. Peter's Basilica, April 18, 2005, www.ewtn.com/pope/words/conclave_homily.asp

14 *An Election Watershed in Chile*, The Wall Street Journal, Dec. 16, 2017, A15

15 *How Blockchain Can End Poverty*, The Wall Street Journal, Jan. 26, 2018, A15

16 *How Blockchain Can End Poverty*, The Wall Street Journal, Jan. 26, 2018, A15

17 *African Leaders Counter Obama's 'Ideological Colonization' in Kenya*, Catholic News Agency, (July 28, 2015)

18 *How Blockchain Can End Poverty*, The Wall Street Journal, Jan. 26, 2018, A15

19 Proverbs 13:22

20 1 Timothy 5:8

21 *What is the difference between Communism and Socialism?*, www.investopedia.com/ask/answers/100214/what-differece-between-communism-and-socialism.asp (January 5, 2018)

CHAPTER 7

FAITH & REASON

Faith and reason are like two wings on which
the human spirit rises to the contemplation of truth;
and God has placed in the human heart a desire to know
the truth – in a word, to know himself – so that,
by knowing and loving God, men and women may also
come to the fullness of truth about themselves.[1]

— POPE SAINT JOHN PAUL

It is an unfortunate truth — but a truth, nonetheless — that most investors don't make very much money in the stock market. The reason is simple, they buy high and sell low. Of course, they know they should be doing just the opposite. They understand that the idea is to buy a stock more cheaply than the price to which it can ultimately rise. Indeed, they would admit that it's foolish to do anything else.

Moreover, when I talk about Warren Buffett's *contrarian* practices or the principles of Value Investing, people have no trouble recognizing the simple truth in what I'm saying. Buffett's approach is so obvious: *Buy when everybody else is selling and driving the price down.* Likewise, Value Investing is no big mystery: *Do your homework, and go with a company that has good management, strong numbers, and sound business characteristics, and importantly, purchase the stock when its price is below its intrinsic value.* What could be more sensible?

Yet, most investors continue to do precisely the opposite. Why? Because they are human beings whose actions are driven by the *psychology* intrinsic to the human condition. Psychology may be the least appreciated aspect of investing. More often than not, people's investment behavior has less to do with the prospects of companies than with what those people assume and believe about their own prospects. Their decision making reflects not so much reasoned choice as it does their confidence or anxiety, optimism or pessimism, and the emotions and conflicts they are experiencing at a particular moment. So, in large measure, the study of investing is about the study of investors.

Jason Zweig, a financial columnist for *The Wall Street Journal*, has delved deeply into the behavior and decision-making patterns of investors. In his book, *Your Money & Your Brain*, he explores an emerging field called *neuroeconomics* which seeks to discover how the human brain functions when confronted with choices about money.[2] Work under way in this field shows considerable promise in applying the techniques of neurobiological analysis to discerning why investors do the things they do. By way of illustration, Zweig reports on studies conducted by neuroscientist Hans Breiter at Harvard Medical School.

Breiter compared neural responses in the brains of cocaine addicts expecting a fix with those of investors expecting to make money from an investment. Breiter found that the patterns of neurons firing in the two groups were virtually identical. He concluded that such an extremely close resemblance suggests that the expectation of reward may have something like "addictive" power. As Zweig explains it:

> Once you score big on a few investments in a row,
> you may be the functional equivalent of an addict —
> except the substance you're hooked on isn't alcohol or
> cocaine, it's money.[3]

The apparent cause is release of dopamine, a brain chemical that among other things, helps us be decisive. Once a person has felt the dopamine rush, they're inclined to want it again. From an investment point of view, this underscores the difficulty of making objective investment decisions, especially after you've experienced success.

Zweig also recounts an experiment designed to measure the impact of fear on investment decision making. The experiment involved a video card game. Participants chose between options that presented varying degrees of risk. The higher the risk, the greater the potential financial reward. Breathing, heartbeat, perspiration, and muscle activity were monitored throughout the game. Zweig participated in the experiment and was surprised to discover that his responses revealed levels of fear he never would have expected from such a game. As the game proceeded, he found himself making lower-risk card selections after having made a series of selections that resulted in losses:

> At first, the printout showed, my skin would sweat,
> my breath quicken, my heart race, my facial muscles
> furrow immediately after I clicked on any card that
> cost me money. Early on, when I drew one card that
> lost me $1,140, my pulse rate shot from 75 to 145 in
> a split second. After three or four bad losses from the

risky decks, my bodily responses began surging before
I selected a card from either of those piles. Merely
moving the cursor over the riskier decks, without
even clicking on them, was enough to make my
physiological functions go haywire[4]

Such research indicates how reactions that exist well below the level
of conscious awareness influence choices we assume are being made
through reasoned assessment. For all of our intelligence and sophistication, we aren't separated from the primal responses that are essential
to physical life. Fear is inherent in us. It is a gift from God intended to
warn us when there is a possibility of danger. It has enabled our survival
as a species. As neuroscientist Antonio Damasio observes, "Money represents the means of maintaining life and sustaining us as organisms in
our world."[5] So the possibility of its loss naturally makes us afraid.

REFLECTIVE JUDGMENT

Zweig says that the challenge investors face is learning to differen-
tiate between *reflexive* judgment (responses that occur automatically on
the neural/physical level) and *reflective* judgment (intentional, logical
choice). He insists that we should never try to detach ourselves from
the signals our brains are sending us — not that we ever really could.
Rather, we should try to recognize those interior functions, rely on
them to alert us when something seems wrong, then keep our heads
and proceed sensibly.

Good advice, but easier said than done. The stock market meltdown
of Fall 2008 and early 2009, arguably the most threatening economic

event since the Great Depression, demonstrated the effect of fear on investor behavior. Typical reactions hardly reflected Warren Buffett's sanguine advice about how this was a great buying opportunity. Whether or not investors gave voice to the sentiment, their neurons were shouting loud and clear, "That's all very good for Warren Buffett. But I want to *sell!*"

At the height of the panic, I heard from a few clients dazed by the carnage, wondering which stocks to dump, or just seeking reassurance. One called with absolute terror in his voice.

"Get me out of everything," he said. "Turn it into cash before it all falls apart."

I counseled patience. "The market will get through this and turn around," I said calmly. "Our funds are perfectly sound."

But he was having none of it. "Are they FDIC-insured?" he asked.

"No," I explained, "the FDIC only insures bank deposits."

"Then I'm cashing out. I can't take it anymore." With his sense of risk aversion raised to such a high level, there was nothing I could do to assuage his fear.

The answer to such panic is *common sense*, which as the old maxim reminds us, really isn't all that common. Webster's defines it as "practical judgment or intelligence; ordinary good sense," attributes we all like to believe we possess. But how quickly you can lose your grip on them when your expectations are suddenly upended. And it isn't only fear of loss that makes one behave irrationally. Anticipation of gain also plays havoc with your ability to see clearly and act sensibly.

BUBBLES AND FRENZIES

Most investors have heard of the famous "Tulip Mania," a great speculative wave that swept the business community of Holland in the early 17th century. Increased public interest in the flower, which had been introduced into Europe from the Ottoman Empire, sent prices of tulip bulbs soaring, setting off wild speculation in contracts to grow them (essentially, an early version of futures trading). At the height of the frenzy in 1637, bulb contracts were said to sell for as much as 10 times a skilled craftsman's annual earnings. Naturally, such a run-up was unsustainable, and the market for tulip futures collapsed, with none of the contracts ever actually being fulfilled. The incident has since served as a lesson about greed and how expectations can become inflated beyond rational judgment.

A century later, investors lost their lace-cuffed shirts over the infamous "South Sea Bubble." In this debacle, Britain's South Sea Company gained trading concessions in the Americas in exchange for assuming government debt run up during the War of the Spanish Succession (1701-1714). Much of this trade — and there really was very little of it — involved transporting slaves from Africa. But excitement about vast wealth to be gained in the New World, and a scheme whereby certain investors (mostly high-ranking British politicians) were guaranteed a buyback of their shares fueled a speculative bubble that drove South Sea stock up tenfold in a year. This prompted the formation of other companies obliquely related to overseas trade, whose stock issues benefited from the frenzy.

In one famous instance, a new company advertised that its activities were secret (eerily foreshadowing the 1990s boom in which investors had no idea what many of the dot-com companies did). By 1720, when the earliest South Sea subscribers were due a return on their investments, it became apparent that the great New World trader was not going to make good on its highly leveraged debt obligations. Isaac Newton, a firsthand observer of the bubble, commented, "I can calculate the movement of the stars, but not the madness of men." A financial crisis ensued, forcing action by the government and the reorganization of the company. (Sound familiar?) This happened to former shareholders of Chrysler and General Motors. Both groups were wiped out in bankruptcy in the wake of the financial crisis of 2008-2009 when the U.S. taxpayers (i.e., the U.S. Government under Barack Obama) bailed out the UAW.

Whenever mentioning U.S. taxpayers, I like to emphasize that I'm referring to those who actually do pay taxes. Drawing from a Pew Research Center Analysis of the most current IRS data (2015), fifty-six percent of the tax base paid 98.6% of all federal income tax. The remaining forty-four percent of the tax base consists of individuals who earn less than $30,000, and two-thirds of these individuals, 44 million people, owed no federal income tax.[6]

These 18th century investors learned a hard lesson about how humans respond to stress associated with investing. Two centuries later, Federal Reserve Chairman Alan Greenspan called this human trait "irrational exuberance."[7] Irrational exuberance applies to investment decisions leading to a financial bubble and to rash decisions that occur when the bubble bursts.

Congress created the Federal Reserve System in 1913 after a series of financial panics. The Fed is the central banking system of the U.S.

and has a dual mandate: maximum employment and stable prices.[8] Regrettably, other than being aware of the "irrational exuberance" factor, there is little the Fed can do to influence this human response. Greenspan offered this perceptive observation:

> It is human psychology that drives a competitive
> market economy. And that process is inextricably
> linked to human nature, which appears essentially
> immutable and, thus, anchors the future to the past.[9]

Over the centuries, with depressing regularity, people have gotten swept up in the mania of the day — be it British railway speculation, the wild margin trading of the late 1920s (resulting in the crash of '29), or the '90s internet bubble — buying without regard to value, and then later regretting their foolishness. Time and again, we've seen how otherwise reasonable, rational, intelligent human beings can lose their heads and their money.

FOLLOWING THE HERD

Why do people behave irrationally in a crowd or in the excitement of a rapidly moving market? Part of the answer surely is simple conformism, the psychology of the "herd." Neuroeconomic research confirms the power of peer influence. Watching others adopt certain practices or try new things offers a certain emotional reassurance. They rationalize that if others are doing it, it must be safe to do. Under such influence, it doesn't matter all that much where the herd is going, as long as they keep moving.

Another methodology for studying investing-related behavior is known as Behavioral Finance. Based on a field of social science research called *heuristics*,[10] it's not unrelated to neuroeconomics, but it takes a somewhat different approach. The term *heuristics* refers to experience-based problem-solving. It explores economic decision making from the perspective of reference points, information assumed to be accurate and relevant, external influences, and the little mental shortcuts we all employ in our daily choices.

Those who analyze financial decision making from the heuristic point of view employ terms such as *anchoring* to describe how people tend to form judgments based on false data and fallacious assumptions. For instance, during the 1990s tech frenzy, it was popular among investors to select internet stocks based solely on price relative to the prices of other internet stocks. Since high-tech issues were so hot (providing the *anchor* or reference point for comparison), the assumption was that any tech stock would go up in price (without regard to the fundamentals) because other tech stocks had gone up so much. The mania was in full bloom in 1999 and 2000. When the bubble burst, tech stocks crashed across the board, many losing 90 to 100% of their market value.

Another fallacy by which investors tend to find themselves misled is the idea that a good company necessarily equates with a good investment regardless of the price. Any company, even a great one, can get overpriced in the market, sometimes extremely so. When the share price exceeds intrinsic value, it will likely be a poor investment. Investors tend to be overly confident in their view of the future. Thus, they pay too high a price for superior historic earnings growth, assuming it will continue indefinitely, and too low a price for substandard earnings growth, ignoring the fact that this too may change.

Because of the tendency for investors to overestimate their fore-casting ability and underestimate the speed with which earnings growth rates can revert to the mean, companies with bright prospects (currently) get their shares bid up to premium prices. Whereas those with temporarily clouded prospects are knocked down to depressed prices, even if they are perfectly solid in all other respects. But as share prices recover — owing to fundamentally good business characteristics — those undervalued stocks offer the prospects for superior return, while stocks of popular companies disappoint as unrealistic expectations result in share price reductions.

This is the "art" behind Value Investing — buying unpopular stocks of companies with temporarily clouded prospects at a discount to their intrinsic value and riding the reversion wave, while avoiding popular stocks with seemingly rosy prospects.

It is possible to pay too much for anything, especially rosy prospects. For instance, Microsoft's share price was essentially flat for 13 years from 2001 to 2014. It just got too high priced (popular) in 1999, when it was selling at over 50 times earnings. Yet during that timeframe, earnings actually increased almost every year. The same thing happened with Walmart. Its price also traded in a fairly narrow range from 2001 to 2011, until the earnings growth caught up to the stock price. This brought the price earnings ratio down to a more realistic level and it was no longer overvalued. Again, price is a critical component in being a successful value investor. Many investors lose sight of that fact. Value Investing is difficult precisely because it requires investors to do what is counterintuitive, unpopular, and out of favor. Unpopular and temporarily depressed stocks will never make for good cocktail party bragging (they lack excitement), but they generally make better investments.

The *good-company-equals-good-investment* assumption is one of those mental shortcuts that interest students of Behavioral Finance. It's another expression of human nature (related to herd psychology) that allows otherwise sensible people to arrive at false conclusions in a fairly predictable manner. And the long, sad history of bubbles and frenzies illustrates how strong it is — even among investment professionals.

Strangely, experienced portfolio managers, whom you'd think would have the knowledge, experience and discipline to resist irrational impulses, can be as susceptible to the promptings of the mob as the casual market dabbler — in some cases, even more so. Despite excellent educations received at Wharton, Harvard, or other sophisticated business schools, as soon as they enter the profession, all too many of them fall readily into a uniform and self-reinforcing Wall Street mode of thinking. Institutional investors make much of their oft-stated intention to outpace the crowd, yet consistently, they seem to prefer behaving just like their colleagues — and it shows in the investment results they achieve.

They tend to make predictable recommendations of comfortable institutional stocks — those with the largest capitalizations, those followed by many other analysts, and those that are most liquid. They buy and sell in virtually identical, large quantities, following lockstep patterns of constant diversification in the clichéd (and mistaken) belief that diversity by itself guarantees good performance. Rare indeed is the institutional investor who would step off the well-worn path to try a less conventional approach. For instance, buying fewer issues in more concentrated positions of really fine companies (which is a favorite strategy of Warren Buffett and other truly great investment managers) can work beautifully.

Most market pros have very little incentive to make contrarian calls. The risk of professional damage looms too great if they should lose with an unconventional style or with a stock selection that is not ratified by popularity among their peers. They recoil at the possibility of being ridiculed, of looking like idiots. Because their aim is a long career in the highly conventionalized world of investments, failing conventionally is preferable to succeeding in an unconventional manner. It's an illustration of herd psychology, par excellence.

THE FAITH DIMENSION

The insights gained from neuroeconomic analysis point to a very interesting line of inquiry. Monitoring and imaging have been used to track bodily responses and neural activity associated with religious practices like prayer and meditation, as well as to chart the physiological effects of ecstatic spiritual experiences and even of faith itself. This research provides much of the information underlying a book published by University of Pennsylvania neuroscientist Andrew Newberg, MD, and therapist Mark Robert Waldman, *How God Changes Your Brain* (Ballantine Books, 2009). I'm not aware that anyone has ever attempted to compare these religion-related studies with research involving investor behavior, but I think it would be fascinating to see what similarities and differences might be observed. This is not frivolous speculation, because in a very real way, investing is a matter of faith. The idea that owning stock is a valid means of increasing wealth requires that you believe things can get better over time. And that is a fundamentally *religious* idea.

A spiritually-minded person would express this assumption as confidence that God is in control and that He desires our betterment. If you don't have such an expressly religious outlook, think of it as believing in the idea of progress — believing that progress is *possible* — a kind of faith in itself, and similar enough to make my point.

Another way of looking at it is: *accepting that the system works* — which is to say, believing that the market will eventually correctly price individual stocks, bringing them to levels that accurately reflect the intrinsic value of the companies they represent. This is a matter of having faith in the collective wisdom of the millions of investors participating in the market, all of whom bring their own capabilities, perspectives, and sources of information into the process.

Once you accept the validity of investing, you have to believe in the prospects of a particular company. I would hope that your confidence is based on solid data, but it still comes down to faith. Of course, you also have to believe in your data, and this in itself can pose a faith challenge that is formidable even for disciplined professionals who do research for a living. My associates frequently express their insecurities about the thoroughness of their company analyses.

I'll ask, "How much information do you feel you've collected on which to base your recommendation?"

"Oh, maybe 80 percent of what I want," is a typical answer.

"Eighty percent is good," I'll tell them. "Go ahead and make a decision."

"But I really wish I had more details," they'll reply. "Maybe I should keep digging."

"What you want is *certainty*," I'll say, "and certainty is impossible. Trust the work you've done, trust your instincts, and make your best judgment. Because the value of that last 20 percent (what economists call the *marginal utility*) won't really add much to the overall picture." (It may even allow an analyst to develop an overly confident view of his analysis.) In other words, once you've learned how to make assessments about the evaluation of companies, and gained a reasonable amount of experience at it, have faith in your *ability* to do so, without wasting time trying to achieve certainty.

Other religious ideas factor into investing as well, foremost among them the concept of eventual reward. Christians have never achieved unanimity in our understanding of how the *justice* of God balances off against His *mercy*. Ever since the Reformation, Protestants and Catholics have argued over what is the exact and proper relationship between acceptance of God's grace and the need for human works in the attainment of Heaven. Yet all believers seem to feel we're called upon to do *something*, and that God, in whatever measure of justice and mercy, will reward us, as long as our *works* reflect our *faith*.

In the realm of investing, the most basic thing we're called upon to do is exercise self-control. We have to accept the idea of *deferred gratification*, denying ourselves the tangible pleasures of spending in the here-and-now, and instead putting our money into these rather abstract instruments called stocks and bonds, which we hope will bring us a greater reward later. We have to believe it's worth the wait (which is a sort of earthbound equivalent to believing in grace). And then we must choose good stocks and bonds, remain attentive to how our investments are performing, and make whatever adjustments are required as circumstances evolve (which is to say, we must exercise *diligence*, the investor's version of *works* in my theological analogy).

All of this is a matter of *counting the cost*, which is the underlying theme in so many of Jesus' parables. If you are not able to commit yourself to these priorities, then investing makes no sense, and you might as well adopt the eat-drink-and-be-merry approach to economic life. Which is the approach a lot of people — being unable to discipline themselves in other ways — take to life in general. All I can advise in either case is that the costs of such profligacy are rather high in the end.

MAKING SOUND DECISIONS

But this, too, is closely related to the unconscious aspect of our human nature — the religious/moral impulse being, in many ways, as sub-clinical as our responses to the prospects of gain or loss, or our susceptibility to influence by those around us. Which brings us back to Jason Zweig and his neurons. How do we come to terms with those troublesome inner responses that seem to have a life of their own and can so readily dash our economic hopes and expectations? The key is impos-ing structure on our decision making — Zweig calls it, *controlling the controllable* — so that we don't find ourselves struggling with important choices while being "whipsawed by the whims of the moment."

Before you venture too deeply into the stock market, it's wise to invoke the ancient Greek aphorism attributed to Socrates: "Know thy-self." Get clear on what your financial expectations are and ask what level of risk you are willing to tolerate. If you are honest with yourself, you might discover you're not as intrepid as you thought, or more will-ing to assume risk than you may have previously thought. This is the sort of self-awareness I believe every investor should try to develop.

Zweig provides a savvy checklist for investors in the form of the acronym, "THINK TWICE."[11] It's a series of wise tips worth quoting:

Take the global view. Keep calm by using a spreadsheet that emphasizes your total net worth — not the changes in each holding. Before you buy a stock or mutual fund, check to see whether it overlaps what you already own.

Hope for the best, but expect the worst. Being braced for disaster — by diversifying [your holdings] and by learning market history — can help keep you from panicking. Every good investment performs badly some of the time. Intelligent investors stick around until the bad turns back to good.

Investigate, then invest. A stock is not just a price; it's a piece of a living corporate organism. Study the company's financial statements. Read a mutual fund's prospectus before you buy.

Never say always. No matter how sure you are that an investment is a winner, don't put more than 10 percent of your portfolio in it.

Know what you don't know. Don't believe you are already an expert. Compare stock fund returns against the overall market and across different time periods. Ask what might make this investment go down; find out if the people pushing it have their own money in it.

The past is not prologue. On Wall Street, what goes up must come down, and what goes way up usually comes down with a sickening crunch. Never buy a stock or mutual fund just because it has been going up.

Weigh what they say. The easiest way to silence a market forecaster is to ask for the complete track record of all his predictions. Before trying any strategy, gather objective evidence on the performance of others who have used it in the past.

If it sounds too good to be true, it probably is. Anyone who offers high return at low risk in a short time is probably a fraud. Anyone who listens is definitely a fool.

Costs are killers. Trading costs can eat up one percent of your money per year, while taxes and mutual fund fees can take another one or two percent. Comparison-shop and trade at a snail's pace.

Eggs go splat. So never put all your eggs in one basket. Spread your bets across U.S. and foreign stocks, bonds, and cash. No matter how much you like your job, don't put all your 401(k) into your own company's stock.

These are excellent guidelines to refer to when you feel the tug or clash of your neural responses. Keeping them before you (perhaps literally, taped to the edge of your computer monitor) can remind you to slow down, take a deep breath, and *think* before jumping into or out of some investment, putting money at imprudent risk, or foregoing a legitimate earning opportunity under the influence of raw emotion.

Hard as it may be to put into practice, Zweig's insight is correct: investors must learn to discriminate between the *reflexive* and the *reflective*. Doing so involves self-awareness and discernment. Train yourself, and then practice, practice, practice. Harvard economist Richard Zeckhauser makes an excellent suggestion along those lines: "Find cheap situations in which you can test your biases. Keep track in a hypothetical world of cheap experiments."[12] Another good bit of advice.

And don't forget, God has programmed our brains to help us survive and flourish. It's up to us to figure out how to use them most effectively. In my experience, the mind works best when aided by faith and reason.

NOTES

1   *Fides et Ratio* (Faith and Reason): *On the Relationship Between Faith and Reason*, Pope Saint John Paul, opening quote (1998)

2   *Your Money & Your Brain: How the New Science of Neuroeconomics Can Help Make You Rich*, Jason Zweig, (2007).

3   *Your Money & Your Brain*, pages 66-67.

4   *Your Money & Your Brain*, page 164.

5   *Your Money & Your Brain*, page 165.

6   *A Closer Look at Who Does (and Doesn't) Pay U.S. Income Tax*, Pew Research Center, Drew Desilver, (October 6, 2017)

7   https://en.m.wikipedia.org/wiki/irrational_exuberance

8   https://en.m.wikipedia.org/wiki/Federal_Reserve_System

9   https://www.google.com/amp.slate.com/articles/business/moneybox/2007/09/margaret_mead_in_a_pinstriped_suit.html

10 *Judgment under Uncertainty: Heuristics and Biases*, a collection of essays and research papers edited by Israeli social scientists Daniel Kahneman, Paul Slovic, and Amos Tversky, and published by Cambridge University Press (2002).

11 *Your Money & Your Brain*, Pages 266-267.

12 *Your Money & Your Brain*, Page 77.

PHOTO GALLERY

Family Circle (circa 1948) – The cradle of both my Catholicism and my entrepreneurial outlook, our household was typical of American Catholic families in the early 1950s, steeped in the values of traditional Christianity and American free enterprise. My parents taught my brothers and me to be honest and hard-working, and always to deliver on our promises. From left, back row, my brothers Bill, Walter, Jr., and Greg; front row, my father, Walter, me at age 4, my mother, Marian. (My sister, Marianne, would come along in 1949.) It was a real "Ozzie and Harriet" upbringing, though despite Mom's resemblance to the mild-mannered Harriet Nelson, she was the resident disciplinarian.

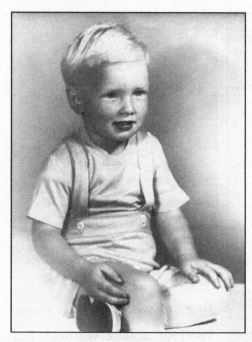

First Portrait –
A two-year-old me.

Ride 'em, Cowboy – My three brothers and I were avid fans of the western heroes so beloved in the 1950s, eagerly following their adventures during Saturday matinees at Detroit's Mercury Theater. At age 5, I got the chance to indulge my cowboy fantasies, when a fellow came to our neighborhood offering pony rides. Looking back, it occurs to me that the pony-ride man was likely one of the first entrepreneurs with whom I came into contact outside my own family.

The Way We Were – (top photos) My 1966 college yearbook portrait records a youthful George Schwartz who today exists only in my mind's eye. But I really did look so fresh and clean-scrubbed once upon a time. Likewise, I recall fondly a perky, young Judith Pearl Arnold — "the smartest girl at Immaculata High School" — who would become my "pearl of great value."

Alma Maters – My years at Detroit's Catholic Central High School were highly formative (top). The Basilian Fathers who ran the school opened my eyes to the truth about abortion. I'm proud to have served on the board of Catholic Central for many years. However, my formal Catholic education began in Precious Blood Parish (bottom), where I attended the local elementary school, now closed.

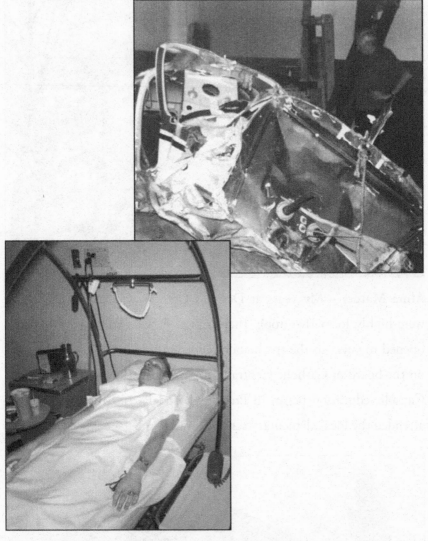

A Challenging Ordeal – An ill-fated flight through a northern Michigan storm left the small plane I was flying in a mangled mess (top) and me with multiple spinal fractures. For months, I lay bound to a Stryker Circle Bed that could tip over to change my position. The experience taught me about what the human body can endure.

Immigrant Roots – My family traces its entrepreneurial tradition to grandparents, Paul & Anna Schwartz, who came to the U.S. from Germany in the early 20th Century. Opa's skill at making condiments launched us on our pursuit of the American Dream, while Oma's experience as a domestic servant instilled an essential respect for hard work which has carried down through the generations (photo circa 1945).

Family Milestone – My parents, Walter and Marian Schwartz, celebrated their 50th wedding anniversary in September 1986. Making it to the half-century mark is a real testament to the sanctity of marriage, a concept that's a factor in Morally Responsible Investing.

My Investing Mentor – While Warren Buffett is 180 degrees away from my views on a number of subjects (especially abortion), the "Oracle of Omaha" is unquestionably a master's master when it comes to investing, and his influence on my professional development has been profound. One of Buffett's great assets in stock analysis is a prodigious memory. I had asked him a question from the floor during Berkshire Hathaway's 1982 annual meeting. At the next year's session I had another question, and was frantically waving my hand to be recognized. Buffett looked at me and said, "Mr. Schwartz, you'll have to be patient; I'll get to you." I was amazed that he'd remembered me from a brief question the year before."

Three Guys with an Idea – The Ave Maria Mutual Funds sprang from the fertile imaginations of three Catholic laymen with a reformist bent, (from left) the late Bowie Kuhn, myself, and Tom Monaghan. Our collaboration proved to be effective. The funds now have more than 100,000 shareholders.

2008 Board Meeting – The Ave Maria Mutual Funds' Catholic Advisory Board (from left): the late Phyllis Schlafly; the late Michael Novak; Lou Holtz; Paul Roney; my colleagues, Tim Schwartz, CFA, and Greg Heilman, CFA, who worked closely with the board; yours truly; and Tom Monaghan. Larry Kudlow was not present for the photo.

CATHOLIC ADVISORY BOARD

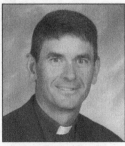

EPISCOPAL ADVISORS

Cardinal
Adam Maida

Archbishop
Allen Vigneron

FORMER BOARD MEMBERS
WHO CONTINUE TO
LEAD AND INSPIRE IN SPIRIT

Bowie K. Kuhn
1926–2007

Phyllis Schlafly
1924–2016

Michael Novak
1933–2017

At a Pershing Financial Advisors' conference in 2011, I was pictured
with Catholic Advisory Board member, Lou Holtz, and my three
sons, Bob, Tim and Mike. Coach is an inspirational and motivational
speaker. I was proud to introduce him as the keynote speaker to over
500 Pershing advisors.

On October 27, 2017, Judi and I celebrated our 49th wedding anniversary
with our five grown children, their spouses and our 10 grandchildren.
We hosted over 200 friends and family at the very same hall at which we
had our wedding reception 49 years earlier, to the day.

Previous Books – My first foray into the world of literary expression was a book titled *Shareholder Rebellion*. Published in 1995, it reflected an activist tendency that would come to fruition in the idea of Morally Responsible Investing. My second book, titled *Good Returns, Making Money by Morally Responsible Investing*, was published in 2010. It helped supercharge the growth of the Ave Maria Mutual Funds.

CHAPTER 8

A CLEAR PRINCIPLE
OF WISDOM

It is above all a clear principle of wisdom
that all progress is truly such if it knows how to add
new conquests to old, to join new benefits
to those acquired in the past — in a word,
if it knows how to make capital out of experience.[1]

— POPE PIUS XII

Experience. Logical progression. Continuity. Building upon judgments and actions whose rightness has been borne out by events. This is the essence of maturity, and it is the perspective which investors bring — or *should* bring — to their task. It does not preclude the taking of risk which is so central to investment decisions. Rather, it helps in calibrating the prudence of the risks at hand. It forces you to focus on evaluating all of the factors involved, and allows you to measure current opportunities in light of the known results of previous choices. It is the antithesis of *gambling*, which is about trying to predict outcomes that are dependent on probability and random chance.

I was a child when Pius gave his wise advice, and I can't say his words made any impression on my second-grader's mind at the time. However, I have certainly built my adult career in accordance with his insights. I do not *gamble* on the stock market or pursue "tips" about "hot" stocks. I do not attempt to "time the market" from day to day. Rather, I seek investment opportunities whose promise can be substantiated by hard data. And while, as the advertising disclaimer always says, "Past performance does not guarantee future results," the success of my methodical and undramatic (some might even say *stodgy*) approach has been demonstrated over time. It reflects the moral wisdom which Pius XII was advocating, it has proven effective in my private investment counseling practice, and it is particularly well-suited to the management of mutual funds.

Indeed, it is true that "a clear principle of wisdom" is to daily proceed with diligent research, careful analysis, patient consideration, and sound judgment. Through the Ave Maria Mutual Funds, we chart our course with clearly stated values and work diligently to "make capital out of experience."

THE ORIGINS OF MUTUAL FUNDS

I became interested in mutual funds early in my career, not least because of their interesting history. The prominence of mutual funds as popular investment vehicles is a fairly recent phenomenon, but the idea of pooling investors has a pedigree going back centuries.[2] The earliest-known instance of recruiting individuals into something resembling a mutual fund occurred in the Netherlands in 1774, when a merchant named Adriaan van Ketwich organized a trust that would invest in bonds from various countries, including Austria, Denmark, the German states, Spain, Sweden and Russia, as well as from colonial plantations in Central and South America.

The Dutch being given to moral aphorisms, van Ketwich adapted the national maxim, *Eendragt Maakt Magt* ("Unity Creates Strength") as the name of the fund, though no Dutch government bonds were included among its holdings. Van Ketwich also set an interesting ethical standard for fund operation by removing himself from day-to-day investment decisions, even while he functioned as the fund's manager. His intention was to avoid the appearance of any conflict of interest.

The success of the venture inspired other Dutch investment projects with similarly edifying names, such as *Voordeelig en Voorsigtig* ("Profitable and Prudent"), founded in 1776 by a group of Utrecht bankers, and van Ketwich's own 1779 follow-up, *Concordia Res Parvae Crescunt* ("Small Matters Grow by Consent"). The Netherlands' King William I was sufficiently intrigued by the potential of pooled investments to sponsor a fund in 1822. The Swiss took up the idea in the mid-1800s, followed by investors in England and other nations, including the thrifty Scotts, who organized investor consortia in the 1880s. Such groups provided a goodly portion of the capital that fueled 19th-Century industrialization. And some of the earliest efforts proved quite durable, van Ketwich's *Voordeelig en Voorsigtig* trust remaining in operation for 114 years.

The fund concept first touched financial life in America when Dutch investors organized to acquire (at a significant discount and a substantial profit) the debt run up by the U.S. government during the Revolutionary War. But the first homegrown American investor pools were the Boston Personal Property Trust, formed in 1893, and the Alexander Fund, organized in Philadelphia in 1907. The Massachusetts Investors' Trust, established in Boston in 1924, was a true mutual fund in the modern sense, with participants holding a range of equities. It was the first of a group of mutual funds that allowed hordes of small investors to participate in the bull market of the 1920s.

The new mutual fund industry took its lumps like the rest of Wall Street in the 1929 crash. But under the close federal scrutiny that came with the advent of the Securities and Exchange Commission (SEC) and a host of government regulations and investor protections, those funds that survived were gradually seen as the way for small investors to participate in the market and gain returns that generally kept well ahead of inflation.

Over the years, different types of funds have appeared — including bond funds, money market funds, index funds, hybrids and others — in response to the demand for asset diversity and to meet a wide array of investor objectives. According to the Investment Company Institute, by the end of 2016, there were more than 8,000 mutual funds worldwide.[3] Mutual funds in the U.S. account for some $21.1 trillion in assets.

VALUE INVESTING

The flagship in my Catholic fund group is the Ave Maria Catholic Values Fund, a name which can be read in two ways. First, because it is based on moral principles advocated by the Catholic Church, it clearly reflects recognizable *Catholic values*. And second, the Fund incorporates the well-established concept of Value Investing. This duality was not inadvertent. I practiced Value Investing long before I started the Ave Maria Mutual Funds. In fact, I would describe myself as a disciple of the world's greatest exponent of Value Investing, Warren E. Buffett.

Those who are familiar with Buffett may see this as something of a contradiction in one who advocates integrating Catholic values and investing. In his private life, Buffett champions causes that are in extreme opposition to the Church's stance on a broad range of subjects. He adheres to an overall liberal social philosophy that, in many respects, deviates from Church teaching. By example, he is one of the largest donors to Planned Parenthood. My attraction to Buffett's investment techniques has elicited quizzical looks on more than one occasion, but I think the explanation I give makes perfect sense — to wit: *"Wayne Gretzky is probably the greatest hockey player in the last 30 years. But what if I found out he was pro-choice on abortion. (In fact, I don't actually know where Gretzky stands on the question.) Would I no longer say he was a great hockey player?* Life is complicated, and conflicting realities can exist side by side. Regardless of my feelings about someone's social views, I could never deny his accomplishments in the area of his professional expertise."

And so with Warren Buffett, I cannot help but admire the manifest business acumen and investing skills that have built Berkshire Hathaway, Inc., his Omaha, Nebraska-based insurance and holding company, into a premier U.S. financial institution. Value Investing is at the heart of this accomplishment, and I have tried to make his approach my own. As I explained the concept in my earlier book:

> Value Investing consists of carefully analyzing all of
> the things of worth in a company, adding them up,
> subtracting the liabilities, and comparing the result to
> the price-per-share at which the company is trading in
> the marketplace. If the company's intrinsic business

value is significantly greater than the market price of its shares, then that company is a logical investment candidate.[4]

The Value Investing method has served Buffett exceedingly well. His investment performance — 20 percent a year over 50 years — has been so spectacular that insurance regulators have permitted Berkshire Hathaway to maintain extraordinarily high levels of equities in its reserve portfolio. The result has been substantially greater reserves than any other insurance firm in the country.[5]

This dazzling performance has been reflected in the heights to which Berkshire stock has appreciated over the years. In early 2018, the Class A shares of Berkshire Hathaway were $320,000 per share. I have benefited directly from Buffett's success, having bought ten shares of Berkshire Class A stock in 1981 at $600 per share. Over a period of three decades, I sold off or gave away nine of those shares, some to pay for college tuition for my five children. I plan to hold onto my one remaining share indefinitely.

Over the years, Buffett has acquired large holdings in such high-profile companies as Coca Cola, Walmart, American Express, U.S. Bank, Wells Fargo, and Burlington Northern Santa Fe. All are well-financed, good companies with good products, and owing to his astute tracking of the market and adherence to Value Investing principles, bought at opportune times when prices were well below intrinsic value. Moreover, Buffett rarely sells a stock, preferring instead to periodically add to his accumulated holdings.

Value Investors like Buffett are not disturbed by fluctuations in the market. You can be sure that all the companies whose shares Buffett has acquired have experienced swings in price during the time he's held them, in some cases quite severe. He sees that as an opportunity, noting that, "volatility is your friend — it allows you to buy low." And overall, Buffett's purchases have trended upward, reflecting the appreciation in the value of the businesses underlying his shares.

Value Investing is thoroughly grounded in the principle of *ownership*. Buffett never thinks of stocks as mere "pieces of paper" or of buying stock as "playing the market." He is a serious investor who understands and appreciates what he owns. Warren Buffett isn't the only investor pursuing the Value approach. Other Value Investors I have admired and try to emulate include: Mike Price of Mutual Shares; Chuck Royce of the Royce Family of Mutual Funds; Bob Rodriguez of First Pacific Advisors; George Sertl of Artisan Partners; Seth Klarman of Baupost Group; Mario Gabelli of GAMCO Investors, Inc.; Bill Nygren of Oakmark Funds; and Donald Yacktman of Yacktman Asset Management. Each of these highly astute investors has an excellent long-term track record.

A great generator of citable observations, Buffett often says he wouldn't care if share prices were totally unavailable for ten years, and the stock market closed down for that time. He's confident that the *value* of his stocks would rise, since they represent ownership of outstanding growing companies.[6] Apropos his Coca-Cola holdings, he has said that if he went to live on some other planet for 10 years, he'd find, when he returned to Earth, that Coke sales had continued to increase.

And his confidence is justified. Buffett does his homework. He's prudent, basing judgments on knowledge previously gained. He exercises great patience in awaiting his opportunities or the "perfect pitch", as he calls it. One might even say that Warren Buffett follows Pope Pius XII's advice by "making capital out of experience."

EVALUATING COMPANIES

How is Value Investing practiced? That is to say, how do you determine whether a particular company represents a good investment opportunity?

In order to answer that, we must first address a very common misuse of terms. Many people — including many investment professionals — speak of the current "value" of a stock, and in doing so, confuse the words *value* and *price*, using the two interchangeably. That is a mistake that can lead to all kinds of confusion (even to losing money in the market). Buffett distinguishes between the two words in this way: "'Price,'" he explains, "is what you *give*, while 'value' is what you *get*." To put it another way, you can purchase a stock at a 50 percent discount from its value, which means its *price* is half its *value* — a good buy, because the price still has the potential to rise. Sometimes the price of a stock exceeds its value, which means the price has already risen beyond any reasonable estimate of the company's value. It's overpriced, and so its price must fall to reach its value.

With this distinction made, there are several statistical methods of assessing the intrinsic value of a business. Three traditional measures are:

1. LIQUIDATION VALUE (LV) — the expected proceeds if a company were to be dissolved and its assets sold and liabilities paid off (a related measure

is 'breakup value,' the combined LV of all the various
components if they were sold off piecemeal).

2. NET PRESENT VALUE (NPV) — the value of
all future cash flows which the business is expected
to generate, discounted back to the present at an
appropriate discount rate (the "discount," being an
adjustment for the purchasing power of the currency
over that period, or what is commonly referred to as
the "time value" of money).

3. PRIVATE MARKET VALUE (PMV) — a
comparison with sale prices when other firms within
the same commercial sector change ownership.
Much like real estate assessors look for comparable
transactions to arrive at an estimate of value, this
is a valuation based upon price comparisons with
transactions in which entire businesses, in similar
industries, change hands.

While all three of these measures are objective, they each involve
comparisons, projections, and assumptions which, by their nature,
are imprecise, indefinite, subject to change, open to interpretation,
and somewhat less than fully tangible (for instance, when trying to
determine PMV, it can be hard to find other companies similar enough
to make true apples-to-apples comparisons). It is an irony of business
that for these standards of valuation to gain in substance and credibility,

they must be viewed in light of something that is even less tangible but absolutely essential in determining the worth of a company: goodwill.

Goodwill is intangible. It involves image, reputation, trust: the relationship between a company and its customers. It is how a business is perceived, thought about, referred to, and depended upon. Goodwill includes public awareness of the company's products or services, and recognition of its brand names and trademarks. It is a firm's standing, relative to the competition. In essence, it's all the things related to human consciousness, appeal, and motivation that are intangible in the extreme, but nonetheless so important that the success of a company — indeed its very survival — depends on them. Goodwill may be intangible, but it is a monetary reality. It's difficult to calculate, but there are many instances where the value of goodwill is the most critical (even the largest) number in the value assessment. It's why you buy Coke instead of just "cola."

No statistical measure can fully determine a company's potential as an investment without considering goodwill — which generally makes Liquidation Value a very incomplete measure of a company's worth. LV is concerned only with the property, hardware, inventory, and cash that remain after a business has ceased operations. It is accounting taken to the far edge of minimalism, a tally of inanimate assets divorced from human action. In a sense, it's a projection of failure, showing you only what you'll have if the business goes belly-up — useful in providing a worst-case perspective, but of limited helpfulness in measuring the potential of a growing company in which long-term investors might wish to put their money.

Net Present Value, on the other hand, does take goodwill into account, because it is based on cash flow, which can only be generated by the interplay of a company and its market (in which goodwill is an essential component). The same with Private Market Value, since PMV measures the worth of an active company against the prices paid for other firms doing business in the same general field.

None of these measures is flawless in its ability to indicate which stocks will rise in price over time. Each can be criticized in various ways. For instance, determining a company's NPV depends on the ability to reliably predict future cash flows — which experience shows often turns out to be an exercise in tea-leaf reading, since the future is infinitely variable. Business conditions change, as do consumer tastes and patterns in customer behavior. Unanticipated problems arise. Important personnel come and go according to shifts in individual circumstances.

What's more, statistical calculations, divorced from other information about a company, can be profoundly misleading. They can put a false appearance of good investment potential on stocks that are actually what Buffett, in his colorful way, calls cigar butts. These are stocks that seem attractively cheap, but unfortunately, wind up staying cheap for years because in reality, the companies behind them aren't well managed, profitable or growing — they lack *good business characteristics*. But if numbers in themselves don't tell the whole story, they do tell quite a lot. Each methodology has its strengths, and they are all arrows in a stock analyst's quiver. Taken together, these techniques allow skillful analysts to paint a useful picture.

Recent years have seen the introduction of a fourth analytical methodology, more refined than Liquidation Value, Net Present Value or Private Market Value, based on the equation:

$$\frac{EV}{EBITDA}$$

This procedure measures a company's Enterprise Value (EV) — its *capitalization*, the total market value of its stock plus its outstanding long-term debt minus its cash equivalents. This figure is divided by the company's gross cash flow, defined as its "EBITDA" (Earnings Before Interest, Taxes, Depreciation and Amortization), to arrive at a ratio. Typically, the lower the ratio of EV to EBITDA, the more attractive the stock price for purchase. Everything else being equal, a company whose Enterprise Value is five times EBITDA would be a better investment prospect than one where EV is 10 times EBITDA.

OTHER CONSIDERATIONS

Beyond the numbers, there are other factors to consider when evaluating prospective investments. For instance, Warren Buffett looks for whether a company has some unique aspect that helps to protect its position in the marketplace from the assaults of competition — what he calls, a moat (as in the moat around a castle). One factor that constitutes a moat is brand equity, the high level of consumer awareness and loyalty that can sustain product popularity over time. In a sense, a brand is the ultimate expression of goodwill. Implicit in a well-established brand is a promise of what will be delivered to the person buying that product — what brings the customer back time after time.

Brand equity would have been an especially compelling factor in Buffett's purchases of Coca-Cola stock. He bought 100 million shares that later split two-for-one twice, so he currently has 400 million shares of Coke in the Berkshire portfolio. Coke is a global icon with market visibility and consumer attachment maintained for more than a century. Coke is often ranked as the world's most valuable brand. It has such a high level of recognition that its trademark elements, the famous cursive-script logo and contour bottle have been altered little since Coca-Cola was first introduced as a packaged consumer product.

You'll likely make good money buying the stocks of companies with super-strong brands — that is, *if* you don't pay too much. Price is the key. And the challenge in acquiring the shares of such companies is generally speaking, price gets down to the "bargain" level only when something goes terribly wrong.

The greatest buying opportunity in the history of Coca-Cola was in 1985 when the infamous "New Coke" was introduced. The reformulation of Coke's traditional ingredient mix (premiered with much fanfare to combat market inroads by other soft drinks, primarily rival Pepsi) so infuriated loyal customers as to cause protests and black-market importation of Coke bottled outside the U.S., where the new version hadn't yet been launched. Coke shares took an uncharacteristic tumble, and anyone who bought at the depressed price was amply rewarded when the original formula was resurrected as "Coca-Cola Classic" and the stock rebounded.

Another factor that can function as a moat is a firm's Unique Proprietary Position (UPP) in its market. A company like Walmart might be said to have a UPP. Walmart stores not only benefit from a well-established brand identity, they are often the only big-box retailers in the communities where they are located (until recent years, mainly in small towns and suburban areas). They offer such a comprehensive array of products at such comparatively low prices that independent competitors find themselves under severe pressure, often to the point of closure. Walmart regularly faces community resistance — right up to mob-in-the-street protests — over that power to revolutionize local economies. So much so that it's become almost fashionable to dislike Walmart, and nearly everyone does — that is, except for the roughly 100 million Walmart shoppers (in the U.S. alone).

Simple market dominance can have a moat-like effect, at least for a while, though the past 25 years or so has demonstrated just how fleeting dominance can be. We've witnessed a series of *wiz-bang* technology firms, each with some impressive new product, system, or process, bursting onto the scene, dominating its market for a time, then being swept aside by some other, even more dazzling digital gizmo (does the name Atari or Blackberry sound vaguely familiar?). Likewise, even venerable firms that were top-of-mind when it came to meeting specialized needs have seen dominance vanish. Remember Pan-Am or TWA, both in their time virtually synonymous with overseas travel? If not, then ask the U.S. car makers how well they're dominating the automotive world these days.

When I was a boy, General Motors had 55 percent of the auto market in the U.S. and was actually threatened with antitrust action by the government because of its near-monopolistic dominance. It was the very model of a profitable, multinational corporation, with AAA-rated bonds in such demand that investors would pay as much for them as for gilt-edged U.S. Treasury securities.

There is at least one factor that can offer some protection of market position — at least for a while, anyway. That is a growing stream of sales and earnings. The key is *trend*. In his stock analyses, Buffett doesn't just look for good current performance, he wants to see the line going up over an extended period of time. That kind of continuing growth, projected against the other measures used in the Value Investing method, can suggest the presence of a moat, marking a good investment prospect.

Related to sales and earnings, of course, is profitability. Buffett is interested in companies with low debt (an *unleveraged* balance sheet). High return on equity means that the company doesn't have to take on debt or issue more stock to raise the capital it needs to refurbish plant and equipment, pay dividends, or make acquisitions. Being debt-free also allows a company to buy back its own shares on the open market.

Truly profitable companies (think Microsoft or Apple) finance their own operations and growth with *free cash flow* (defined as profit plus depreciation expenses that are in excess of maintenance and capital expenditures). This shows that a company can pay its own way — a sign that it likely has good business characteristics and, especially, good management. I have always stressed the importance of owning shares of financially strong companies, a view which has been vindicated by the 2008–09 recession.

Such financial powerhouses — usually debt-free, with highly liquid balance sheets — have control of their own destinies in ways that leveraged companies do not. The overleveraging of corporate America has been well documented. During the economic prosperity of the 90s, many companies leveraged their financial structures with loads of debt. Before the financial crisis of 2008-2009, banks adopted the practice in the form of *subprime* lending.

When business is good, leverage can be an effective strategy. Taking on debt allows a company to exploit earning opportunities that yield a greater return than would have been possible without the debt. The problem comes when things slow down. All that borrowing means interest expense that takes a huge bite out of profits already adversely affected by contracting revenues. In late 2009, as the U.S. economy emerged from the worst recession since the 1930s, investors were once more awakening to the dangers of excessive corporate debt and, conversely, to the benefits of being debt-free.

Debt-free companies have a much greater ability to weather economic storms, even continuing to grow stronger during recessions. They can continue to make investments in capital improvements, as well as research and development for new products. They can expand through acquisition of properties, products or entire businesses, often buying from distressed sellers at bargain prices. If their own stock is depressed because of short-term market factors, they can use cash reserves to repurchase their own shares on the cheap. Because of their staying power, strong companies can opportunistically steal customers from the weak, putting nails in the coffins of their faltering competitors. Financially powerful companies use recessions to build for the future and enhance, if not guarantee, earnings growth when prosperity returns, advantageously using liquid resources during periods of general economic weakness to create permanent shareholder value.

In contrast, companies that are overburdened by debt — the financial weaklings — have trouble managing cash flow. They are forced to cut back on capital expenditures and R&D, hurting their competitive positions with long-term detrimental consequences. They often find themselves forced by their bankers to make drastic cuts in spending, personnel and product planning, or else they resort to the stopgap measure of raising equity capital at the worst possible time, diluting shareholders' interests.

While low debt is never an absolute guarantee that a company's stock is a good investment, it is almost always a characteristic of a high-quality company. Usually, it is a residual of a really good business with proprietary products and good profit margins, operating in a growth market and blessed with good management. And when the shares of such fine companies are out of favor and depressed, they can be superb investments.

Another factor that rates high in Buffett's assessment of potential investments is demonstrated integrity among corporate managers — having to do with the ethical standards by which a company is run. Are the company's managers forthright and open in their dealings with shareholders? Buffett values candor. Does executive compensation accurately reflect company performance? Managers getting rich at the expense of the shareholders — rather than as a justified consequence of demonstrated success — is a red flag. Consistent with his views on compensation, Buffett never issues stock options to Berkshire Hathaway executives. Rather, he's known for paying his people well, giving them ample bonuses, and encouraging them to buy Berkshire stock on the open market with their own after-tax dollars, just as any other investor would.

The most important factor in shopping for stock, of course, is price, and that's always a moving target. Buffett is the archetype of the *contrarian* investor. He buys world-class companies that are well managed and have strong finances, but that are temporarily out of favor. He took a big position in Wells Fargo, the banking and financial services company, back in the '90s, when banks faced severe problems and S&Ls were blowing up everywhere. At the height of 2008's wildest market fluctuations, when investors were running in circles from pure panic, Buffett wrote an op-ed piece for The *New York Times* in which he offered a bit of strikingly contrarian advice:

Buy American! I am.

A simple rule dictates my buying: Be fearful when
others are greedy, and be greedy when others are fearful.
And most certainly, fear is now widespread, gripping
even seasoned investors. To be sure, investors are right
to be wary of highly leveraged entities or businesses
in weak competitive positions. But fears regarding
the long-term prosperity of the nation's many sound
companies make no sense. These businesses will indeed
suffer earnings hiccups, as they always have. But most
major companies will be setting new profit records 5,
10 and 20 years from now.[5]

Naturally, timing is critical to the success of Buffett's contrarian practices. A good buy isn't a good buy forever, only when conditions make it so. And conditions never stay the same. Life goes on. But Buffett would insist that trying to "time" the market is a loser's game. There are speculators who sit in front of computer screens all day long, jumping in and out of closely followed stocks trying to make a quick turn on the movement of a point or two. But such people are gamblers, not true investors.

ROOTS OF THE APPROACH

As *I* follow the principles of Warren Buffett, so *he* was influenced by Benjamin Graham, his mentor at Columbia University's Business School in the 1940s. Graham co-wrote, with Columbia colleague David L. Dodd, the classic investment text, *Security Analysis*, considered the seminal work of the Value Investing philosophy. First published by Whittlesey House, a division of McGraw-Hill, it has been updated several times. I'm pleased to own a leather bound limited-edition copy with a foreword by Buffett. On one of my trips to Omaha, I was able to have him sign it.

Appearing in 1934, the book drew on lessons learned in the 1929 stock market crash and the then-unfolding Great Depression:

> Graham and Dodd chided Wall Street for its myopic
> focus on a company's reported earnings per share, and
> were particularly harsh on the favored 'earnings trends.'
> They encouraged investors to take an entirely different
> approach by gauging the rough value of the operating
> business that lay behind the security. Graham and
> Dodd enumerated multiple actual examples of the
> market's tendency to irrationally under-value certain
> out-of-favor securities. They saw this tendency as an
> opportunity for the savvy.[6]

Security Analysis built on a long tradition of attempting to apply empirically verified analytical techniques to investing judgment which had reached its zenith with publication of the "Dow Theory" in 1902. Created by Charles H. Dow, co-founder of *The Wall Street Journal*, the theory maintained that stock prices could be charted — and thus, buying and selling decisions made — by tracking three types of price activity. As explained by Dow's protégé, William Peter Hamilton, who further refined the theory:

> Simultaneously in any broad stock market there are
> — acting, reacting and interacting — three definite
> movements. That on the surface is the daily fluctuation;
> the second is a briefer movement typified by the reaction in
> a bull market or the sharp recovery in a bear market which
> has been oversold; the third and main movement is that
> which decides the trend over a period of many months,
> or the main true movement of the market.[18]

Dow's theory had a "macro" perspective, based as it was on the Dow Jones Averages, the composite index of selected railroad and industrial stocks he had created. While the effectiveness of Charles Dow's theory as a market predictor has been questioned and various other stock indexes have appeared on the scene, the Dow Jones Industrial Average remains the most common, general-purpose measure of market performance. Its daily closing figure is still the first answer given to the question, "How did the market do today?"

Graham and Dodd, on the other hand, focused on achieving a

more definitive assessment of the particular strengths and weaknesses of individual corporations, whose prospects might contrast dramatically with general market performance.

At bottom, *Security Analysis* stands for the proposition that a well-disciplined investor can determine a rough value for a company from all of its financial statements, make purchases when the market inevitably underprices some of them, earn a satisfactory return, and never be in real danger of permanent loss. Warren Buffett, the only student in Graham's investment seminar to earn an A+... made billions of dollars by methodically and rationally implementing the tenets of Graham and Dodd's book.[7]

So indeed he did. And throughout my own career, I have attempted to profit from Buffett's example and the insights he gained at the knee of Benjamin Graham — to "make capital out of experience," as it were. I like to think Pope Pius XII would be pleased.

Warren Buffett's one "religious" reference (at least, the only one of which I'm aware) expresses a great financial truth in a humorous way: "The market, like the Lord, helps those who help themselves. But, unlike the Lord, the market does not forgive those who know not what they do." In other words, investing successfully requires information. More to the point, it requires thorough and specific information. I related a very telling anecdote in one of my earlier books:

> Going to Thanksgiving dinner at a friend's house one
> year, I mentioned I'd bring a couple of bottles of very nice
> Nouveau Beaujolais. My friend said, "Oh, if it's that nice,
> can you bring me a case? I'll set some aside." But the fact

is Nouveau Beaujolais must be drunk in the year it was bottled — usually by mid-December of that year — or it turns to vinegar. I brought my friend some Cabernet Sauvignon instead. She knew enough about wine to know that some of it improves with age, but she didn't know enough to realize that Nouveau Beaujolais is an exception. People make the same kind of mistakes with investments every day.[8]

It's like the old saying, "A little knowledge is a dangerous thing," as all too many market dabblers have discovered to their chagrin.

Digging out the facts on which to base sensible investment decisions takes hard work. I have a staff of Chartered Financial Analysts (all of them with MBAs) pursuing information on prospective investments all day every day. They read annual reports, press releases, 10Ks and 10Qs (government-required disclosure forms), are all highly educated, highly trained, talented, motivated (well paid) and experienced. They analyze balance sheets and income statements, contact managements, and visit selected corporate headquarters and branch offices. They attend conferences where company managers make investor presentations, and then they sit down with those executives for face-to-face interviews in breakout sessions. Then, all this primary research is supplemented by secondary research obtained from national brokerages and regional boutiques.

BASIC GUIDELINES
This is security analysis done at a high level of sophistication. But

whether or not individuals avail themselves of such professional service, there are guidelines of which they should be aware. Inspired by Buffett and distilled over my 50 years in the field, these are the basics, a few simple precepts that can at least point you in a productive direction when you're making investment decisions.

1. ERR ON THE SIDE OF CONSERVATISM.
Don't let hope or optimism color your reading of
the facts. If anything, understate your assessments.
For instance, if you're attempting to estimate value
by applying the traditional measures, LV, NPV and
PMV, use the lowest of the three, or a low average
with emphasis on NPV. As Benjamin Graham advised,
leave a margin of safety — a large margin (think of it
as building a bridge strong enough to carry a 30,000-
pound truck, but then only being willing to drive a
10,000-pound truck over it).

2. KNOW THE FIELD IN WHICH YOU
WISH TO INVEST. Over the years, my firm has
concentrated on businesses we know well. We've
had a particular interest in financial services (banks,
thrifts and insurance companies), healthcare, auto
aftermarket companies, and manufacturers of certain
proprietary products. Buffett calls it operating within
your sphere of competency.

3. CHECK OUT YOUR OWN BACKYARD.

Any number of investment opportunities can present themselves right in your own area, and proximity makes it easier to get to know the folks minding the store. Since we're headquartered in suburban Detroit, we frequently go out and "kick the tires" of companies we're following in Michigan or the adjoining states of Indiana and Ohio. To quote the famous sermon, sometimes there are "acres of diamonds" in your own backyard.[9]

4. BE A CONTRARIAN.

You can't possibly know when is the "perfect" time to buy, but if you're minimally aware of trends, you can make reasonable projections. It's like the old saw about buying straw hats in January, when they're cheap, in anticipation of making a profit selling them when demand is up in July. We made a great contrarian investment for our clients some years ago, at a time when healthcare was looming as an issue on the political horizon. It was a Michigan company called MEDSTAT, which did outcomes analysis for healthcare organizations. We realized this service would be increasingly important, but at the time, MEDSTAT's principal asset, its database, didn't even appear on its balance sheet. We started buying shares and were rewarded years later, when the stock soared as the result of a buyout by a

Canadian company. The return for our clients was
more than six times their average costs.

5. BE PATIENT. Value Investing is like farming.
You cultivate, you sow, you water, and then you wait.
It takes time before the crop comes in. Likewise,
the Value Investor needs farmer-like patience and
persistence — which I can tell you from years of
personal experience. We make investments just about
every day, but we sell only occasionally. As in the
MEDSTAT example, above, eventually you reap
the harvest.

To sum up, investing is not gambling. It's work — *hard* work —
and you will make mistakes doing it. But with seriousness, maturity,
dedication, and a willingness to take risks, you can succeed and "make
capital out of experience."

NOTES

1   *Christmas Address*, Pope Pius XII, (1952)

2   K. Geert Rouwenhorst of the Yale School of Management's International Center for Finance, provides an excellent capsule history of how mutual funds came onto the financial scene in his paper, "The Origins of Mutual Funds" (2003), available online from the Social Science Research Network (http://papers.ssrn.com/sol3/papers.cfm?abstract_id=636146).

3   ICI 2017 Investment Company Factbook at p. 170 & 174 (www.ici.org/pdf/2017_factbook.pdf).

4   *Shareholder Rebellion*, Page 15.

5   *The New York Times*, October 16, 2008.

6   http://en.wikipedia.org/wiki/Security_Analysis_(book)

7   http://en.wikipedia.org/wiki/Security_Analysis_(book)

8   *Shareholder Rebellion*, Page 17.

9   "Acres of Diamonds," by Rev. Russell H. Conwell (1843-1925), Baptist minister, lecturer, and founder of Philadelphia's Temple University.

CHAPTER 9

GOOD RETURNS

America, it is said, is suffering from intolerance. It is not. It is
suffering from tolerance: tolerance of right and wrong, truth and
error, virtue and evil, Christ and chaos. Our country is not nearly so
much overrun with the bigoted as it is overrun with the broadminded.[1]

— VENERABLE ARCHBISHOP FULTON J. SHEEN

Investors' reactions to the Ave Maria Mutual Funds range from very negative to resoundingly positive. Some folks will reject the entire concept of Morally Responsible Investing out of hand. They may recoil from anything that smacks of religion, Catholic or otherwise. They may be thoughtlessly enamored of "a woman's right to choose." Or they may assume that any sort of non-economic screening criteria must necessarily present an insurmountable obstacle to investment success. Whatever their preconceptions, they are unlikely ever to be part of our shareholder community.

At the other end of the spectrum are those who burst with enthusiasm as soon as they hear about our funds. Perhaps they're naturally disposed toward projects with a Catholic (or at least a spiritual) character. Perhaps they're fiercely committed to the pro-life cause — in which case, surprisingly enough, some don't even care all that much about the investment results.

In between those two poles is a large group of people who could be prospects for our funds, if they were convinced that what we have to offer is valid — that Morally Responsible Investing really is effective in the service of both conscience and investment success. It is these folks I've had in mind while writing this book. After all, most people are interested in making money, whatever their religious affinities. Likewise, most people are moral in their business dealings, so there is something inherently intriguing about the idea of tying investments to a larger moral vision.

I have found this to be especially true in my dealings with institutional investors. The people who manage institutional investments are charged with obtaining good performance. It's incumbent upon them to exercise due diligence. They must carefully examine the track record of any fund under consideration, and investigate the people running it. No one with such a fiduciary responsibility is free to choose a mutual fund merely because it's Catholic, not even those managing investments for Catholic organizations.

However, most investment professionals are aware that their financial choices do not exist entirely apart from the missions of the institutions they represent. This has been a significant advantage to us in gaining entry to the inner circles of decision making within some of the nation's most respected foundations and charitable groups. The result is that over 500 institutions, mostly Catholic, have invested anywhere from $10,000 to $100 million in the Ave Maria Mutual Funds. That's a substantial testament of faith in the MRI concept. It's especially significant because it reflects the judgments of people whose professional lives are spent evaluating every conceivable type of opportunity. It hasn't happened by accident. My colleagues and I have had to make our case. We've had to explain our investing process and prove that it works.

INVESTMENT RESEARCH IS CRUCIAL

In contrast to much financial-services marketing these days, our presentation does not depend on propagating any illusions of mystery about what we do. We don't invoke the razzle-dazzle of impressive, technical-sounding jargon. We make no pretensions to special insights, nor do we imply secret access to "inside information." And we do not claim superior skills with which to *time* the market (let me say it again: market timing is mostly a loser's game). Actually, we make it plain that our methods are quite simple and transparent, based mostly on hard work.

An important advantage we *do* have — one that allows us to make investment decisions that are both financially astute and morally appropriate (and the one which most individual investors *don't* have) — is institutional investment research. As a mutual fund management company, Schwartz Investment Counsel, Inc. has the resources to acquire sophisticated research services. We utilize information provided by a variety of leading Wall Street firms and regional boutique brokerage houses in assessing the investment merits of thousands of companies. The data acquired from such sources, added to the work of our own analysts, provides the basis for sound professional judgment in mutual fund management.

Separately, in following the moral guidelines established by our Catholic Advisory Board, we use a proprietary screening process developed by our firm which includes outside sources. Our approach, Morally

Responsible Investing, often gets lumped in with what's called ESG (environmental, social and governance) factors. These include corporate policies and practices bearing on such concerns as energy use, political contributions, labor and human rights issues, and other items relevant to mutual funds that have ethical interests. Most of these ESG criteria are the province of the "socially responsible" funds. And the scope of information available is astounding.

Incidentally, between 5 and 10 percent of companies whose stocks are held by most mutual funds, including the largest and most widely marketed, would not pass Ave Maria's moral screens.

INVESTMENT STRATEGIES

We have five different Ave Maria Mutual Funds, each with a distinct investment objective and strategy consistent with the designated objective:

Ave Maria Value Fund
Ave Maria Growth Fund
Ave Maria Rising Dividend Fund
Ave Maria World Equity Fund
Ave Maria Bond Fund

The Ave Maria Value Fund (formerly Ave Maria Catholic Values Fund) focuses on companies believed to be undervalued relative to their intrinsic worth. The Ave Maria Growth Fund consists of mid-cap and larger companies that offer above-average potential for growth in revenues. The Ave Maria Rising Dividend Fund invests in companies that have a long history of paying and increasing dividends. The Ave Maria World Equity Fund consists of companies of all capitalizations from around the world. The primary investment goal of these four funds is long-term capital appreciation. The fifth fund, the Ave Maria Bond Fund, invests in investment-grade debt securities of domestic issuers, including the U.S. government and its agencies and instrumentalities, corporations, and money market instruments. The Bond Fund's primary goal is the preservation of principal while also generating a reasonable level of current income.

The Funds do not invest in companies believed to offer products, services, or otherwise engage in practices that are contrary to core values and teachings of the Roman Catholic Church. The Catholic Advisory Board sets the criteria for screening out companies based on moral principles. In making this determination, the Catholic Advisory Board's members are guided by the Magisterium of the Roman Catholic Church. This process will, in general, avoid four major categories of companies:

1. those involved in the practice of abortion
2. those whose policies are judged to be antifamily, such as companies that distribute pornographic material
3. those that contribute corporate funds to Planned Parenthood
4. those engaged in embryonic stem cell research

FUND PERFORMANCE

Combining this depth of corporate intelligence with the security analysis principles of Value Investing discussed in Chapter Seven allows us to identify issues that can be productive additions to our portfolios. In the Morally Responsible Investing approach, *value* and *values* really are complimentary concepts. When we complete our fundamental security analysis, believe we have identified a company that has good business characteristics (and all the other criteria we're looking for), and determine that the valuation is reasonable, we check to see if the company is an offender before we buy its securities in any of the Ave Maria Mutual Funds.

Since its inception on May 1, 2001, through December 31, 2017, the Ave Maria Value Fund has produced an annual return of 6.98%. Meanwhile, the Ave Maria Growth Fund has produced an annualized rate of return of 11.25% versus 9.81% for the S&P 500, since its inception on May 1, 2003. And in the ten-year period ended December 31, 2017, it had an annual return of 9.41%, versus 8.5% for the S&P 500. The Ave Maria Rising Dividend Fund produced an annualized return of 9.49% from its inception on May 2, 2005, through December 31, 2017, versus 9.07% for the S&P 500 over the same time period.

I believe that the future investment performance of the Ave Maria Mutual Funds may continue to be superior to that of the market in general, and whatever the future results may be, will be done in a morally responsible way.

PROFESSIONALISM SHOWS

The good investment management practices, solid fundamental

research of our team of analysts, and execution of sound investment strategies must be counted as factors in the excellent performance. But if I had to highlight one single reason we have done so well, I think it would be this: We keep our investment goals and our moral aims in balance. As I have said many times, especially whenever I have been interviewed by the media, my staff and I are not theologians, nor do we hold ourselves out as experts on Church teaching. We are investment professionals, a group of CFAs and MBAs with many years of experience in managing other people's money. We depend on the guidance of our Catholic Advisory Board, which is composed of prominent Catholics, some of whom have theological credentials, but all of whom are loyal to the Magisterium. So we have plenty of moral fire power when it comes to Catholic theology and doctrine, especially as it relates to pro-life and pro-family matters.

This separation of financial objectives and philosophical commitment is not apparent in most "socially responsible" funds, nor even in other religiously inspired funds with a moral purpose. A conversation I had some years ago with the manager of an Evangelical mutual fund brings this point into focus. The fund had been designed specifically to avoid, among other vices, investments in alcohol-related stocks. And such was the manager's dedication to eradicating "evil rum," as he put it, that financial returns were a distinctly secondary consideration. "Alcohol has destroyed so many lives and hurt so many people, it's ruining the world," he said. "This is my mission, and I believe in it with all my heart."

He was a truly devoted Christian man, but he was a poor mutual fund manager, and that lack of expertise was reflected in the poor performance of his fund. We, on the other hand, are intensely concerned about investment performance and want to produce the best returns possible for our shareholders. We believe that is the best way to accomplish our religiously inspired mission. We have been practicing Morally Responsible Investing for several years, and it has worked!

Questions have been raised about applying Morally Responsible Investing to direct management of institutional investment portfolios. Some Church organizations that have invested in our funds — particularly some dioceses — have inquired about the possibility of crafting individually tailored investment portfolios to meet their specific investment objectives. I believe this is perfectly practical, since we can readily draw on the systems and procedures already in place and functioning so well for our funds. Consequently, we have developed what are called Separately Managed Accounts for institutional clients. A Separately Managed Account has a lower expense ratio associated with it, as little as half of what we charge to manage our mutual funds. But it requires a correspondingly higher minimum level of participation — much higher: $25 million, as opposed to the $2,500 mutual fund minimum commitment.

NOTES

1　*Old Errors and New Labels*, (Chapter 7, *A Plea for Intolerance*), Venerable Archbishop Fulton J. Sheen (1931).

FROM MANY
ONE

America is the only nation in the world that is founded
on a creed. That creed is set forth with dogmatic and even
theological lucidity in the Declaration of Independence;
perhaps the only piece of practical politics that is also theo-
retical politics and also great literature. It enunciates that
all men are equal in their claim to justice, that governments
exist to give them that justice, and that their authority is
for that reason just. It certainly does condemn anarchism,
and it does also by inference condemn atheism, since it
clearly names the Creator as the ultimate authority from
whom these equal rights are derived.[1]

– G. K. CHESTERTON

A creed presents core beliefs; explains the *why* — the *raison d'etre*
(*reason for being*). Business consultant Simon Sinek says that thriving
entities begin with *why*. His TED Talk is one of the most viewed of all
time — 7.4 million viewers and counting.[2] According to Simon, thriving enterprises begin with *why*, and then proceed to *how* and *what*.

America began by focusing on *why*. The Declaration of Independence describes *why* the colonists severed ties with the Kingdom of

Great Britain and concludes with 56 signers pledging their lives, their fortunes, and their sacred honor.[3] That same day, the Continental Congress named a committee to design a Great Seal — a symbol that would convey the *why* of this new nation and would appear on all official papers and documents.[4] John Adams, Benjamin Franklin, and Thomas Jefferson were the first committee members, but the task ultimately involved three committees, six years, and fourteen members.[5] The committee unveiled the Great Seal in 1782, a year before the Revolutionary War ended. The seal included the phrase *E Pluribus Unum* (*From Many One*), a captivating phrase that served as the nation's unofficial motto for nearly two hundred years. A mere two decades before the nation's Bicentennial, Congress declared *In God We Trust* as the official motto.[6]

Both *In God We Trust* and *From Many One* go to the heart of who we are as a nation. We are a melting pot of people who celebrate our cultural diversity and traditions while also pledging allegiance to the United States of America as one nation, under God. We are from many one. We hold certain truths to be self-evident — that all are created equal and endowed by their Creator with certain unalienable rights including the right to life, liberty, and the pursuit of happiness. Through the years, patriotic songs, eloquent speeches, and compelling monuments have expressed these powerful and timeless truths. Importantly, economic principles and investment fundamentals have played, and always will play, a pivotal role in the fulfillment of these truths.

A stable economy — characterized by private property and the free exchange of goods and services — makes possible the pursuit of happiness for the broadest number of people. It is through ownership of property that the human soul experiences a responsibility to steward and sustain. This awareness awakens a healthy pride of ownership that in turn stirs a striving for excellence. The freedom to own encourages entrepreneurial activity, spurs discovery, emboldens dreams, secures liberty, celebrates accomplishment, rewards creativity, and contributes to a culture of growth, sustainability, life, and health. As my friend and Catholic Advisory Board member Larry Kudlow frequently says, "Free market capitalism is the surest path to prosperity."

One hundred fifty years before the Declaration of Independence, investors in England and the Netherlands shared this timeless entrepreneurial spirit, this conviction, this faith, this belief in human ingenuity and trust in God. These investors made a pivotal decision. They funded the Mayflower's voyage, and their investment changed the world. Their investment made possible the founding of the United States.

The year was 1620. Dutch and British investors gathered resources in support of the Pilgrim's maiden voyage. The proposed crossing required incredible courage, perseverance, and faith. A painting in the United States Capitol rotunda honors this spirit.[7] The painting depicts the Speedwell, a ship that initially accompanied the Mayflower.[8] On the sail, we read "God With Us."[9] This was the Pilgrims' motto and would later be modified to "In God We Trust" and become the nation's. Three hundred and thirty-six years after the Mayflower's landing, Congress adopted it as the motto for the United States of America. Where would we be without the commitment of those who funded the Pilgrim's voyage... the investors... the capitalists?

Perhaps one day a painting depicting the investors who made the Pilgrims' voyage possible will appear in the Capitol Building. They deserve to be recognized. A closer look at the real history behind the Pilgrims' experience is enlightening. Historian Charles A. Beard's *Basic History of the United States* reveals:

> Under English law all the territory claimed in America belonged to the Crown. The monarch could withhold it from use, keep any part of it as a royal domain, or grant it, by charter or patent, in large or small blocks, to privileged companies or persons.

And so, when the Pilgrims decided to leave England for political, economic, social or religious reasons, they had to get permission. As farmers and working-class citizens they had little if any capital. So they approached a group of private capitalist entrepreneurs who were interested in exploiting the new world for profit, especially gold. As historian Robert V. Remini explains in *A Short History of the United States*, this group "formed a joint-stock company, the London Company, in which shares were sold to stockholders for twelve pounds ten shillings [roughly $250] in order to sponsor colonization by settlers in North America." The London Company then obtained a grant from the Crown and additional financing through the Merchant Adventurers which considered their investment as a loan to the Pilgrims to be paid back, with interest and a share of the profits. Upon landing, the Pilgrims considered themselves as bound in a "common course" to repay the loan as quickly as possible... the Pilgrims "were more like shareholders in an early corporation than subjects of socialism." Richard Pickering, deputy director of Plymouth Plantation, said the plan "was directed ultimately to private profit."

The irony, then, is that the part of history most frequently left out not only ignores the Pilgrims' failed experiment with collective farming, but also the fact that it was private capitalists, risk-taking entrepreneurs, hoping to gain a profit from the venture, who were the ones who funded the start of America. As another historian, Steve Wiegand noted:

> Part of the charm of U.S. history is that many of the images it conjures up are based on things that never really happened. Many historians are appalled at the acceptance of myths as fact by so many Americans...
>
> It should be comforting that this really happened: the land of the free and the home of brave was initially funded by capitalists hoping to turn a profit. How delightful.[10]

The spirit of adventure, invention, reasoned risk-taking, and investment that has come to characterize the best of American culture also inspired those who invested in the founding of what eventually became the United States.

When economic and investment decisions remain free of undue government interference and unwise tax policies, the United States is truly a land of opportunity. How then do we account for the rise of socialism in the United States? Socialism is the opposite of investment capitalism. Socialism shuns private ownership and empowers government. Many who believe in socialism seek to do good by redistributing wealth. This is unwise on many levels. Moreover, socialism is not sustainable. As

Margaret Thatcher famously quipped, "The trouble with socialism is that eventually you run out of other people's money."[11] Something has to give. Quality drops and a shortage of goods and services ensues.

But there is also a subtler point. Socialism weakens and eventually drains the human spirit. When one owns something, one innately takes better care of it. One accepts responsibility. When one is given something, that spirit of responsibility either does not exist, or exists in miniature. For example, in general, people take better care of a car they own versus one they rent. Similarly, in general, less litter exists in neighborhoods of homeowners than in areas of public housing. Socialism dehumanizes and is incongruent with the human soul. That is why socialism has never worked and will never work.

By contrast, capitalism rewards innovation and fosters honesty, industry, and respect for the dignity of all human beings. Capitalism rewards virtue and *virtue equals strength*.[12] Strength of character aspires to excellence in all things. With virtue, life is a journey of discovery; a daily commitment to making good and healthy choices, recognizing that some decisions involve sacrifice, delayed reward, and sometimes the reality that the goodness of the decision may be the only reward.

Government programs that provide a safety net for specific, temporary circumstances are helpful, but problems occur when the safety net becomes a culture of dependence. Too often the dependence results from unhealthy choices and decisions made contrary to virtue. The choice might be to take drugs, view pornography, or engage in sex outside of marriage. Unfortunately, government programs sometimes incentivize these choices. Public policies and government programs should always begin with consideration for the dignity of the human person and the best interests of marriage and the family. Sadly, too often the opposite occurs.

In 1964, President Lyndon Johnson ushered in the modern welfare state. He sought to build the Great Society, but instead set in motion an expensive, tragic, downward spiral — particularly among urban families and neighborhoods. The Great Society is the "largest, most intrusive expansion of federal power ever."[13] The Great Society illustrates socialism's many deficiencies. Massive government programs operated by distant and largely unaccountable bureaucrats is a recipe for waste, fraud, and failure. Some perspective:

> Fifty years after most of the Great Society programs
> were cemented into place, it's almost impossible
> to measure the damage they inflicted on the most
> vulnerable marriages and families in the United States.
> This is perhaps the most dismal legacy of the Johnson
> years, and a sad testament to the vision of social
> planners who believed more government would mean
> stronger families and marriages...
>
> by incentivizing government funding of single mothers
> who did not marry the fathers of their children, and
> by expanding the panoply of welfare state programs to
> Americans who were already experiencing serious stress
> and hardship, a series of significant problems became a
> tangle of pathologies...

A plague of fatherlessness ensued, leading to nearly
72 percent of all American black children being
born without married parents by 2015. Marriage has
become a rare and distant thing…

Did it have to be this way? When Johnson came to office
in late 1963, more than 90 percent of all American babies
had married parents…

Today, more than 40 percent of all Americans are
born to unmarried mothers. More than three of every
10 children live in some arrangement other than a
two-parent home. Cohabitation continues to climb,
and has become the acceptable norm for millions of
Americans. The most recent Census Bureau report says
barely half of all American children are living with
both married biological parents…

Poverty and single-mother households were both higher
after the Great Society than before, and the number of
intact families experienced significant decline…

The consequences of broken families and widespread
poverty are profound. Reliable sociologists and
demographers, liberal and conservative alike, concur
that children from broken family structures are
far more likely to become involved in crime as

intergenerational dependence on government grows...

William Simon Foundation President James Piereson,
who has studied urban issues for decades and cogently
analyzed the 1960s, has concluded: "The scores of
burned-out, crime-ridden, and bankrupt cities in
America today must be counted as part of the legacy of
the Great Society."[14]

Do we have the resolve to change course? Do we have the wisdom
to reign in this unwise and perhaps unconstitutional expansion of
federal power? Do we have the courage to face socialism, both as it
exists and as it is being proposed?

This book attempts to make connections between religious faith
and financial prudence. Unquestionably, politics impinge on both,
and perhaps that's inevitable. America was born largely out of human
strivings that are religious at the core, and those strivings continue.
Over the centuries, masses of people have come to these shores to
worship in freedom, improve their lives, and live in a country that aspires
to *equal justice under law.* And the form of government matters greatly.
In the United States, government derives its power from the consent of
the governed. Separation of powers and enumerated roles set forth in
the Constitution provide a basis for course correction when government
goes astray. The interplay of faith, marketplace, and government is at
the heart of the American story, and it always will be.

SOCIALISM

It was something of a shock to read the headlines about a spring 2009 *Rasmussen Reports* opinion poll in which a razor-thin majority of respondents (only 53 percent) declared their preference for capitalism over socialism. How could it be — twenty years after the fall of the Berlin Wall and the collectivist, police-state nightmare it had so long symbolized — that Americans weren't more convinced about the virtues of an economic system that thwarted the world-domination aims of the "Evil Empire?" Had the recession so shaken our confidence? Were we really so shallow and thoughtless as a people? Were memories that short?

Parsing the poll numbers more closely, it becomes apparent that age played a significant part in framing the 53 percent figure. Respondents under age 30 favored capitalism only 37 percent to 33 percent, with 30 percent undecided. At the same time, 49 percent of those in the 30-something age group went for capitalism, against 26 percent for socialism, a considerably wider spread. The 40-plus crowd was in favor of capitalism overwhelmingly; only 13 percent went for socialism. Not surprisingly, investors as a group preferred capitalism by a margin of five to one, while 25 percent of non-investors had a warm spot for socialism.[15]

It was frequently asserted, back during the days of the Cold War, that the United States and the Soviet Union were basically "two sides of the same coin." This view has persisted stubbornly in certain intellectual and creative circles, despite all evidence to the contrary. The leftish intellectual establishment has portrayed the U.S. and U.S.S.R. as essentially the same. A book titled, *Scorpions in a Bottle*, published in 1989 by Hillsdale College Press, consists of a series of presentations examining misperceptions about the struggle with totalitarian communism. It features marvelous insights from William Bennett, Sidney Hook, Jeane Kirkpatrick, Irving Kristol, Melvin Lasky, Michael Novak, and other perceptive observers of the period.

It's fascinating to see how certain "deep thinkers" continue to deny that there is anything uniquely virtuous in America's way of life. Since the Soviet Union took its much-deserved place in history's dustbin, the "moral equivalence" argument has been given a wider focus in effort to dismiss all suggestions that the United States offers greater personal freedom or economic opportunity than other societies. This in spite of the fact that downtrodden people from all over the world continue to "vote with their feet" by emigrating from their oppressed home countries to America.

What the 2009 *Rasmussen Reports* opinion poll actually reveals is the extent to which the distinctions between capitalism and socialism — two inherently conflicting visions of personal and economic liberty — have been blurred by mass media and an educational system given over to the false notion of *moral equivalence*. People too young to have seen the reports of Soviet oppression, and those whose understanding has been dulled by propaganda of the *Why-can't-we-all-just-get-along?* variety are least likely to recognize as unique and indispensable the system that has brought the United States its unparalleled freedom and prosperity. In fact, they have only the vaguest notion of what capitalism and socialism are — a truth made evident by an earlier poll that noted a full 70-plus-percent favorable rating for a "free-market economy" (as opposed to "capitalism"). How you phrase the question matters.

Make no mistake: socialism is not a "third way" of organizing economic life. It is, in fact, merely a lesser degree of government centralization than Soviet communism. Economies are distinguished by who owns and controls property and resources — as Marx put it, the "means of production." Either *people* are the owners (individually or as corporate groups), or *governments* are the owners. Ownership by people allows for the exchange of assets, which makes goods and services available through payments of money or other units of value. Producers profit, and consumers obtain the things they need and desire. Ownership by government, or the imposition of stifling government regulation, subsidization, or production "priorities" disrupts free exchange, or precludes it altogether.

This is a critical point. The capitalist system provides a variety of incentives for people to produce things which other people are willing to pay for. When government is the producer — or even when government interferes with transactions between producers and consumers — incentives are reduced or destroyed, production declines, and scarcity increases. This is not only an economic failure; it is a moral failure, because human needs are not met.

DEMOCRATIC SOCIALISM

Whenever and wherever socialism has been tried, it has failed. Unfortunately, this immutable fact does not deter committed socialists. They contend that with refinement, socialism can work. One such refinement involves placing the word "democratic" before socialism. Clearly, a name change does not change the substance. Michael Novak observed:

Democratic Socialists are eloquent about visions of

virtue. Yet they seem to me nostalgic and wistful
about political and economic institutions... They are
hostile to capitalism, but vague about future economic
growth... Their measures invariably enlarge state
power... to regard a dreamy socialism as beneficial
and humane, is to ignore dozens of historical examples.
The record of existing socialisms is plain, and so is
the prognosis of future socialisms. Whatever the high
intentions of its partisans, the structures they build
by their actions promise to increase poverty and to
legitimate tyranny.[16]

Novak's insights echo those of Winston Churchill, perhaps the most insightful statesman of the 20th Century and one of the finest statesman of all time. Churchill could have retired as a hero following Germany's surrender in May 1945. He served with distinction and led Great Britain through their most perilous time; their *Darkest Hour*.[17] With wit, words, and conviction, he defeated the world's most ominous dictator. Following the war, he detected a threat potentially more pernicious — the creeping advances of socialism. The British people, having survived the brutality of war, yearned for an ideal, serene world. They were susceptible to the alluring call of socialism, a false security offered by nationalized medicine and "cradle to grave" welfare.[18]

Churchill recognized the danger. The bloody war had just ended, but the battle for the soul of England was just beginning. A way of life weighed in the balance. Churchill decided to deliver a nation-wide broadcast. He spoke with courage, candor, and kindness. His words expressed the tender wisdom of an elder statesman. He was 70 years old:

> I declare to you, from the bottom of my heart, that no
> socialist system can be established without a political
> police… No socialist government conducting the
> entire life and industry of the country could afford
> to allow free, sharp, or violently worded expressions
> of public discontent. They would have to fall back
> on some form of Gestapo, no doubt very humanely
> directed in the first instance.[19]

It seems no degree of charity, consideration, or carefully chosen words could insulate Churchill from the hurt feelings triggered by his candor. Even members of his family questioned his judgment. To this day, the left lampoons Churchill's address as his "crazy speech."[20] And yet, clearly Churchill was right. He understood that liberty can be lost through bad ideas, even when advanced by well-intentioned people. He had the courage to speak the truth. He knew that he would pay a price, and he was swept out of office.[21] But, he did not flinch.[22]

A SOCIALIST RUNS FOR PRESIDENT

The 2016 campaign for president of the United States marked the first time that a declared socialist came close to winning the nomination of a major party.[23] Hillary Clinton ultimately won the Democratic Party nomination with more than 15 million primary votes, but Bernie Sanders, a self-described "Democratic Socialist" and active in politics as a socialist for decades, garnered more than 12 million votes. [24] Not long ago, the election of a "Democratic Socialist" as President of the United States would have been unthinkable. In 2016, more than 40% of Democrat primary voters supported Bernie Sanders. Encouraged by this support and promising a "political revolution," Bernie plans to run again in 2020. [25] If successful, he would be 79 years old when sworn in as President of the United States.

How does an intelligent person, let alone 12 million Americans, fall for socialism? One's formation plays a significant role. Bernie's formation reveals the prominent and persuasive role of higher education, public policy, and mass media. Bernie Sanders began at Brooklyn College, and then transferred to the University of Chicago at a time when the University of Chicago was well known for having prominent faculty who preferred socialism over capitalism. He soon became an activist and graduated in 1964 with a degree in political science. Sanders has been a politician ever since.

> Multiple socialist student groups also existed at the school, and renowned political theorist Hannah Arendt spoke on campus about the conditions needed to spur revolution. In October 1962, David Stark Murray, president of the Socialist Medical Association, talked to students about the fight for socialized medicine — a Sanders platform since his first political post as mayor of Burlington, Vt., in the early 1980s. [26]

In 2015, Millennials (those born between approximately 1980 and

2000) [27] surpassed Baby Boomers — 75.4 million Millennials v. 74.9 million Baby Boomers.[28] A 2016 poll reported that among Millennials under thirty, socialism scores higher than capitalism — 43% viewed socialism favorably, compared to 32% who viewed capitalism favorably.[29]

A battle for the hearts, minds, and votes of young voters has been underway for years. Cementing a college student's political worldview, particularly concerning non-negotiables such as abortion, can set a person's voting pattern for life.[30] During the 2016 presidential primaries, some sought to soften socialism's stigma by referring to "democratic socialism." One Millennial's perspective:

> Millennials suppose that the qualifier "democratic" refutes worries about socialism. To them, worries about growing government, higher taxes, and unfeasible policies are only so much condescension from older generations who have a phobia of things they don't understand. My peers think democratic socialism is a happy idea embraced by blond, bike-riding Scandinavians, not a concrete system requiring a byzantine, tyrannical bureaucratic apparatus and potentially radical lifestyle changes.[31]

Socialism opposes private ownership, imposes centralized policies, and requires centralized control. Centralized policies necessarily involve centralized control and eventually police power to enforce the centralized policies. This tragic and predictable cycle only benefits the socialists at the top, the government leaders living lavishly while encouraging citizens to economize.[32]

Human ingenuity is a nation's most precious natural resource.[33] Unlike socialism, capitalism incentivizes achievement. Free enterprise, free speech, private property, entrepreneurship, and Morally Responsible Investing encourage creativity. Prosperity hued by ingenuity rather than inhibited by bureaucracy provides the surest path to sustainable development.

DEMOCRATIC CAPITALISM

Democratic capitalism is the opposite of democratic socialism. Indeed, the definition of *socialist* includes its antonym, *capitalist*. Socialism emphasizes state control, bureaucracy, and intervention. Capitalism stands for liberty, limited government, and private ownership. Michael Novak put it this way:

> What do I mean by "democratic capitalism"? I
> mean three systems in one: a predominantly market
> economy; a polity respectful of the rights of the
> individual to life, liberty, and the pursuit of happiness;
> and a system of cultural institutions moved by ideals
> of liberty and justice for all.[34]

Socialism views human beings as instruments of the state. Capitalism views human beings as masterpieces, created in the image and likeness of God. To socialists, human beings have value when they are useful. To capitalists, there is nothing more valuable than the human person. Socialists seek the completion of tasks assigned by the state. Capitalists seek the fulfillment of opportunity emanating from an unending horizon of discovery and from every human being's inherent ingenuity.

Capitalism protects and promotes liberty, providing an environment that extends equal opportunity to all and that encourages all to pursue their talents, hopes, and dreams. Morally Responsible Investing is a manifestation of this spirit. Diligent research, sound judgment, and character rooted in virtue provide a winning formula for achieving good returns. Novak's "three systems in one" description of democratic capitalism provides a framework for further consideration; namely the market economy, a government respectful of rights, and cultural institutions.

1. A market economy leads to a higher standard of living. Through competition, products and services improve as do value and quality. Through competition, those who "build a better mousetrap" reap the rewards for having done so. They sell more mousetraps. They become the industry standard, at least until a competitor creates a new, improved, and often less expensive option. When this occurs, that person receives the reward of market share. A percentage of the market shifts to the new product. These forces incentivize and reward the conditions that lead to a full and happy life, one that includes goals and rewards.

For a market economy to thrive, marriage and families must thrive. Lawrence Kudlow has served as a member of our Catholic Advisory Board since 2005 and recently was named White House National Economic Council Director. He put it this way:

> The greatest economic challenge of our time is how to
> restore economic growth. Over the past dozen years,

average real growth has slowed to 1.8 percent annually, under both Republican and Democratic presidents and congresses. It's a bipartisan problem...

While restoring economic growth may be the great challenge of our time, this goal will never be realized until we restore marriage...

In short, marriage is pro-growth. We can't do without it.[35]

Societies flourish by providing conditions for individuals, families, and communities to thrive. Every person brings a unique combination of talents and dispositions. Where their life goes depends much upon how they develop, dedicate, and apply their talents, the choices they make, and the character they demonstrate day in and day out. Free markets enable families to flourish.

2. By "a polity respectful of the rights of the individual to life, liberty, and the pursuit of happiness," Novak means a system of limited government with checks and balances against the potential for abuse of power. There has never been a more ingenious, wise, and productive system of government than that established by the founders of the United States. The Constitution takes into account the fallen nature of the human condition and recognizes that power corrupts. Knowing this, the framers divided power among the three branches of government. One of socialism's fatal flaws is its failure to take into account the fallen nature of human beings. This flaw stems from socialism's failure to see

the human being as made in the image and likeness of God. The Constitution wisely takes into account human nature and rightly provides a system of checks and balances. These checks and balances contribute to achieving what Novak refers to as "a polity respectful of the rights of the individual."

3. Cultural institutions constitute the third of the "three systems in one" description of *democratic capitalism* provided by Novak. Cultural institutions rely upon a healthy economy. The for-profit world provides the funding that enables the nonprofit world to exist. Taxes can only go so far. Cultural institutions depend upon the generosity of those who have succeeded in the world of finance, business, trade, and transactions. Without the financial success of individuals, families, businesses, and corporations, the wealth needed to finance cultural institutions would not exist. Taxes collected by the municipal, county, state and federal governments first fund essentials such as roads, public safety, public schools, the legislature, the courts, the executive branch, drinking water, and waste management. After directing taxes to cover these core government functions, what remains to support cultural institutions? Not enough to enable cultural institutions to thrive; but enough when blended with private funding and charitable donations.

A strong economy provides the optimal way to achieve prosperity and a higher standard of living for all. To this point, Novak observed:

> A dynamic economic sector is the poor's best hope of
> escaping the prison of poverty. It is the only system...

to take poor people and make them middle class and some of them even (*horrors!*) rich.[36]

Democratic capitalism enables an economy that builds sustainable, efficient, and high quality goods and services while rewarding virtue and fostering integral human development. Socialism can never do this and never really intends to do so.

The push for socialism will dominate politics for decades to come. The Democratic Party stakes their future on votes generated through government expansion and politicizing race, economic policy, and immigration. In essence, the Democratic Party has become the party of socialism. But socialism is no substitute for the ingenious balance of power and limited government set forth in the United States Constitution. Socialism always leads to oppression and wealth redistribution, and too often results in tyranny. Socialism cannot match capitalism in the context of the economy and is no match for democracy in the context of sound government. Winston Churchill put it this way: "Democracy is the worst form of government, except for all the others."

VIRTUE = STRENGTH

The miracle that became the United States of America shines bright when we remain faithful to the virtue, wisdom, practical politics, and timeless truths presented in the U.S. Constitution and animated by the nation's founding document, the Declaration of Independence. Our shared future depends upon our integrity, including our willingness to faithfully and meticulously abide by the Constitution.

Socialism is inconsistent with the U.S. Constitution. Unfortunately, "the school of legal realism" — the dominant strain within legal education[37] — and the politicization of the courts pose a grave danger to America.[38] Socialism can never fulfill the promise that emanates from the Declaration of Independence and the U.S. Constitution. Socialism looks at life through a different lens. Where capitalists see opportunity, socialists seek control. Socialism's fundamental flaw flows from its failure to see the human person as made in the image and likeness of God. We were thereby made to be free to create, dream, produce, and cultivate rather than submit to government programs that ultimately undermine the dignity of the person and decimate the desire to grow in virtue.

Virtue equals strength — strength of character, strength of marriages, strength of families, and strength of schools, society, and culture. By living virtuous lives, we inspire others. In the words of St. Mother Teresa, do "small things with great love."[39] Our happiness flows from the liberty to make good decisions and to persevere in faith. From this place of virtue, we gain greater appreciation for our nation's unofficial and official motto. We trust in God as we overcome obstacles, pursue goals, and celebrate that we are all in this together — we are from many one.

NOTES

1   https://www.goodreads.com/quotes/262437-america-is-the-only-nation-in-the-world-that-is; https://www.chesterton.org/america/

2   https://startwithwhy.com

3   https://www.redstate.com/diary/sunshinestatesarah/2012/07/04/we-mutually-pledge-to-each-other-our-lives-our-fortunes-and-our-sacred-honor/

4   https://en.wikipedia.org/wiki/Great_Seal_of_the_United_States

5   https://origins.osu.edu/history-news/god-we-trust-or-e-pluribus-unum-american-founders-preferred-latter-motto

6   https://en.wikipedia.org/wiki/E_pluribus_unum; *America's God and Country, Encyclopedia of Quotations,* William Federer at 175 (2000)

7   https://www.aoc.gov/art/historic-rotunda-paintings/embarkation-pilgrims

8   www.pilgrimhallmuseum.org/ap_voyage_mayflower_speedwell.htm

9   *America's God and Country, Encyclopedia of Quotations,* William Federer at 85 (2000)

10 https://www.thenewamerican.com/culture/history/item/4797-who-funded-the-mayflower

11 https://www.snopes.com/politics/quotes/thatcher.asap

12 The expression "virtue equals strength" is the motto of SportsLeader. https://www.sportsleader.org/

13 http://www.theamericanconservative.com/articles/lbj-vs-the-nuclear-family/

14 https://www.focusonthefamily.com/socialissues/citizen-magazine/what-has-the-great-society-wrought

15 *Rasmussen Reports,* Thursday, April 9, 2009.

16 *The Spirit of Democratic Capitalism,* Robert Novak, 27 (1982)

17 https://en.wikipedia.org/wiki/Darkest_Hour_(film)

18 https://en.wikipedia.org/wiki/History_of_the_National_Health_Service_(England)

19 https://www.hillsdale.edu/wp-content/uploads/2016/04/Arnn-2015-Lion-to-the-Last.pdf

20 https://www.cambridge.org/core/journals/journal-of-british-studies/article/winston-churchills-crazy-broadcast-party-nation-and-the-1945-gestapo-speech/69173E13972975F7FD31A0A8F7621890

21 https://en.wikipedia.org/wiki/United_Kingdom_general_election,_1945

22 https://www.nationalreview.com/2015/01/lion-last-larry-p-arnn/

23 https://www.vox.com/policy-and-politics/2017/8/5/15930786/dsa-socialists-convention-national; https://www.vox.com/cards/bernie-sanders-issues-policies/bernie-sanders-socialist; http://www.politifact.com/truth-o-meter/article/2015/aug/26/bernie-sanders-socialist-or-democratic-socialist/

24 https://www.realclearpolitics.com/epolls/2016/president/democratic_vote_count.html

25 *Bernie Sanders is Showing How He'd Run Against Trump in 2020,* Eric Bradner, CNN, February 3, 2018.

26 *Can Sanders' Civil Rights Experience at U. of C. Translate on Campaign Trail?* Jasper Craven, Chicago Tribune, August 26, 2015.

27 http://thefederalist.com/2016/02/15/why-so-many-millennials-are-socialists/

28 http://www.pewresearch.org/fact-tank/2016/04/25/millennials-overtake-baby-boomers/

29 http://thefederalist.com/2016/02/15/why-so-many-millennials-are-socialists/

30 *More Immigration Would Mean More Democrats,* National Review, Jason Richwine, October 3, 2017.

31 http://www.nationalreview.com/article/431455/sanderss-democratic-socialism-millennials-love-it

32 http://www.dailymail.co.uk//article-2075066/Obama-family-jet-Hawaii-separately-cost-100-000-taxpayer.html

33 *The Human Mind Is Our Most Precious Commodity,* Marian Tupy, FEE Foundation for Economic Education, February 13, 2017.

34 *The Spirit of Democratic Capitalism,* Robert Novak, 14 (1982)

35 *Marriage is Pro-Growth: The Economy Can't Do Without It,* Larry Kudlow, Faith Matters, Issue 3.

36 *The Spirit of Democratic Capitalism,* Robert Novak, (1982)

37 *The Moral Foundations of Republican Government,* Edwin Meese III, *Imprimis* (September 1986)

38 *The Tempting of America: The Political Seduction of the Law,* Robert Bork (1990)

39 https://www.goodreads.com/quotes/329513-god-does-not-require-that-we-be-successful-only-that

CHAPTER II

SOUND
ADVICE

The greatest gift we can receive or pass on
is the opportunity to find and pursue our passion,
and in doing so, to make a difference
by helping others improve their lives.
To be truly rich is to live a life of meaning.[1]

— CHARLES G. KOCH

Schwartz Investment Counsel, Inc., exists to help clients improve their lives through sound investments and to do so in a manner that does not offend their core beliefs. Morally Responsible Investing provides the peace of mind that comes from knowing that one's investments do not support pornography, abortion, Planned Parenthood, or embryonic stem cell research.

Founded in 1980 and headquartered in Plymouth, Michigan, Schwartz Investment Counsel, Inc., provides investment counseling services to families, trusts, retirement funds, foundations, endowments, corporations and mutual funds. We are committed to providing sound advice based upon sophisticated research, prudential thinking, and our experience. Our clients benefit from the firm's key tenets:

- focus on long-term, mutually beneficial
  relationships
- strong commitment to fiduciary responsibility
  and prudent investing to meet clients' investment
  objectives while remaining consistent with their
  risk tolerance levels
- diligent application of fundamental security
  analysis and strict discipline to provide continuity
  and stability to investment portfolios

Since our investment management style is conservative and long-term, there is no basis for an advantageous short-term relationship with clients. This long-term approach enables us to avoid short-sighted, short-term performance mania and undue portfolio risk assumed by those who strive for maximum short-term appreciation. We pursue long-term goals including preservation of principal, income generation, and growth of capital consistent with clients' risk-tolerance levels. We manage accounts in a prudent manner utilizing trust-quality investments. Our approach seeks to provide clients with above average returns through investments in entities that have strong business characteristics and below average risk. We look for entities with a stock price lower than what we believe is the entity's intrinsic value. Making these determinations requires diligence, research, skill, and professional judgment. I am very proud of our team of investment professionals.

A CONVERSATION

I have had the privilege of being interviewed on radio and television

many times through the years. Raymond Arroyo, Host of EWTN's
The World Over, has been particularly supportive. As an illustration
of the perspective and advice that Schwartz Investment Counsel, Inc.
provides, I present the following exchange from a broadcast to millions
of viewers worldwide conducted on December 14, 2017:

> *The U.S. economy is riding high. What's causing it and
> how will the markets and your pocketbooks be affected?
> With analysis, I'm joined by the founder and portfolio
> manager of the Ave Maria Mutual Funds, George
> Schwartz. George, the Tax Reform Package will lower
> the corporate rate down to 21% from 35%. What
> impact might that have on the economy?*

> It's going to be positive for almost everyone, Raymond.
> There may be a few quirks that hurt the highest
> income earners. But apart from that, it'll do a lot of
> the things that President Trump has been talking
> about. That is, help the middle class. It's going to help
> corporations with that very sharp reduction in the
> corporate rate. It will make them more competitive
> in the world market and the increased profits can be
> invested in creating jobs, adding plants and equipment,
> and I think this will help the middle class dramatically.

> I'm a longtime believer in supply side economics as
> preached by my good friend Larry Kudlow, who's a

member of our Catholic Advisory Board. He's been pushing the White House to move in this direction.

George, Larry Kudlow has gone on record saying he didn't consider this a real tax reform package because it raises rates on the upper income as you just said a moment ago. Supply side economics is all about cutting taxes so that those in the upper brackets will then invest and start businesses. If you're raising the personal rates, won't that do the opposite?

It's not a perfect package. Clearly. On the other hand, it's not a package that looks like it was written by liberal, socialist leaning Democrats either. It'll have benefits, but not as great as Larry would have liked. Larry has pushed for reduction in corporate tax rates. And that's the key phraseology. Corporate tax rates. Dropping from 35% to 21% will be very positive for consumers, for investors, for corporate America, and for working men and women. And I think it will supercharge the stock market and the economy.

The economy is doing well, as you mentioned. Corporate profits are probably going to be up 13% this year, and based on the tax rate cuts, probably another 15% in 2018. A lot of that will flow to benefit Americans across the board.

The estate tax was not included in this program. But the estate tax deduction will be doubled. Is that good enough for you. Should the estate tax have been repealed?

I think it would have been ideal if the death tax was repealed all together. It doesn't raise all that much money and only affects a pretty limited number of people. The wealthy people who are most affected by death taxes or estate taxes have already been taxed six ways from Sunday throughout their life and to have to pay taxes again after they die is ridiculous in my view.

George, in your analysis of this tax bill, what impact will this have upon investors? People that invest in funds like yours, Ave Maria Mutual Funds that seek capital gains. Will this hurt them or help them?

Well, it's not finalized. One provision is harmful to long-term investors. That's the provision that's going to require individual investors to sell stocks on a FIFO basis, First In, First Out. So the oldest shares they bought of a particular issue have to be the one's sold when they start taking profits. For a long time, people have been able to select which lots they want to sell of a particular issue to their tax benefit. If that provision is in the final version of the bill and it becomes law, that will be a negative. Not a terribly drastic thing, but it will be a negative.

Last time you were on the show in April George, the Dow was hovering somewhere around 18,000. It is now moving toward 26,000. Is that kind of growth sustainable? It has broken record after record and risen to places no one ever expected it to go.

As I've told you before so many times over the years Raymond, nobody can outguess the short-term moves in the stock market, and only a fool tries to do that. But throughout the Obama years, the market went up and people would say to me, "Gee Obama must be doing a pretty good job. The stock market is going up a lot." And I used to always say, and still say that if it wasn't for Obama's negative policies the market would have gone a lot higher during the Obama years. And actually now with President Trump in there it's continuing to go higher and I think it will go higher based on the policies of tax reform. Based especially on the policies of deregulation.

Under the Obama administration, the Democrats really had the foot of government on the neck of capitalism. They stifled capitalism and hurt capitalism with regulations, especially regulations,

but also high taxes and an unfavorable attitude
towards growth and the economy.

So with President Trump in there now, he's unwinding
a lot of those things and removing the foot of
government off the neck of capitalists, and we're
starting to see the benefit of that in the stock prices.
And if this tax reform is as good as I think it is, and
it's not great, but if it's as good as I think it is, it's going
to boost corporate profits and probably stock prices in
the New Year. No guarantee of that because nobody,
including me, can outguess the near term swings of
the stock market.

But the trend is up, and long-term investors should
do well in well managed companies, American well
managed companies, like the companies we have in the
Ave Maria Mutual Funds. These Funds are up, by the
way, between 15 and 25%. And that may not happen
again in the New Year, but maybe it will, who knows?

*Here's the big question. As you look at the trend — and
you've been looking at this for a long time, you've been
watching this market go up and down — with it riding
at these stratospheric numbers, is now the time to get out
or to get in? What would you advise people?*

I've said it before, and I'll say it again. Any day is a good enough day to buy a good enough stock and a good enough mutual fund. And don't try to guess the near-term swings. I don't think the stock market is a bubble. One portion of the stock market is a bubble, and that's the index funds; the so-called passive investing mania.

That is a situation where money has flowed out of actively managed mutual funds into the so-called passive investments or index funds and index ETFs (Exchange Traded Funds). And those things are managed in a way that if they get another billion dollars into an index fund they just have to buy the same stocks and the ones that are the big capitalization stocks — the so-called FAANG stocks (Facebook, Amazon, Apple, Netflix and Google) keep going up because those index funds keep buying them. They are high priced. We own none of those stocks in our Mutual Funds on a valuation basis, plus the fact that they're all offenders because they all contribute to Planned Parenthood, the biggest provider of abortions in the world. So we don't invest in those for those two reasons.

I've been reading in so many of these financial publications that people are dumping millions of dollars

*into bitcoin, these cryptocurrencies, what is essentially
internet currency. Your thoughts on this. A wise move,
or risky given that it's not regulated anywhere yet by
governments around the world?*

I think it's not only risky Raymond, I think it's
foolish. That is a bubble. Bitcoin is a bubble. The
price has been up more than a 1000% just this year.
And I don't think it's a currency at all. I think it's a
speculative vehicle. I would avoid it like the plague. I
think it's going to zero eventually. I don't know when.

*It's essentially a worthless commodity, if you will. It's just
the race to invest in it that's driving the price up. Not the
thing itself because there's nothing there.*

There's no intrinsic value, and it does attract drug
dealers and other criminals that don't want to have
their financial transactions monitored or traced. It's
a mania. It's a bubble. It's not an investment by any
stretch of the word.

*George, we're getting a lot of emails from people who
are saying they want to get into the market. A new year.
I'm sure you see a big boost in the New Year because it's
when people begin to invest. They think about starting
anew. This is the year I make a difference in my life.*

What is the proper breakdown between stocks, bonds,
mutual funds, and blue chip stocks? What would you
advise people?

It all depends upon the individual Raymond. It
depends on their age and their investment objectives.
Historically, for the average person, the mix of roughly
70% stocks and 30% bonds is a pretty good mix. And
the stock portion — the equities or equity mutual
funds — is the portion that will give you the capital
appreciation over time, especially if they're well
managed funds like our Ave Maria Mutual Funds.
And the bond portion, whether that's in individual
bonds or in bond funds, gives you the stability portion.
The bond portion should not be viewed as a capital
appreciation vehicle, even though for the past thirty
years bond prices have gone up as interest rates have
gone down. But that's starting to change right now.
Interest rates are starting to go up, bond prices will
be declining, especially the long maturity bonds. The
bonds in our bond fund, the Ave Maria Bond Fund,
are very sort maturity bonds and very high quality and
would be not as nearly susceptible to rising interest
rates as most long maturity bond funds.

George, there are some who look at a fund like yours and
say, "Now wait a minute. The heart of this thing is morally

responsible investing. Not necessarily the investment that's going to give me the most bang for my buck at the end of the day. What would you tell them? Do the two go hand in hand or are there times when they are opposed, making a good return and responsibly investing your money?

We practice what we call Morally Responsible Investing. That means we follow the advice of our Catholic Advisory Board. That Board has asked us to screen out companies related to abortion. Companies that perform abortions like the secular hospitals. Insurance companies that pay for abortions. And so forth. Also, they've asked us to screen out companies that engage in embryonic stem cell research. Companies that contribute money to Planned Parenthood. And companies engaged in the distribution or production of pornography.

So we screen those companies out, and it only screens out about 150 companies out of the Russell 3000. About 5% of the companies. Our analyst and portfolio managers have had no problem getting very good investment results with the 2,850 companies in the Russell 3000 that do not offend theses core principles of the Catholic Church.

And people ask sometimes, "Well how can you get

good investment results if you have to operate with
one hand tied behind your back?" And that's not the
case. Most of those 150 companies that we don't want
to buy aren't ones that we would have wanted to buy
anyways for fundamental reasons. They either have
too much debt on their balance sheets, or are poorly
run, or have a bad business plan, or just are not good
companies. So we've been able to run what we call
clean portfolios without offending these core principles
of the Catholic Church and produce good investment
results for our 100,000+ shareholders.

Excellent. George Schwartz, thanks so much for being here.
If you'd like to know more about Morally Responsible
Investing visit www.avemariafunds.com or you can give
them a call — 866-Ave-Maria; 866-283-6274.
George Schwartz, thanks again.

THE CATHOLIC ADVISORY BOARD

The Catholic Advisory Board sets the criteria for screening out companies based on objective moral truths and religious principles. The companies considered for investment in the Funds are screened using a proprietary screening process developed by my firm, the registered investment advisory firm Schwartz Investment Counsel, Inc. The members of the Catholic Advisory Board are:

PAUL RONEY, *Chairman*
Executive Director of the Ave Maria Foundation and
President of Domino's Farms Corporation.

ROBERT P. GEORGE, PH.D.
Legal scholar, political philosopher and public
intellectual who serves as the McCormick
Professor of Jurisprudence at Princeton University.

SCOTT HAHN, PH.D.
Theologian, Biblical scholar, and author
who serves as a professor at Franciscan
University in Steubenville, Ohio

LOU HOLTZ, *Emeritus*
Former head football coach at the University of
Notre Dame, author and motivational speaker.

LARRY KUDLOW
White House National Economic Council Director
and former member of the Reagan Administration.

THOMAS MONAGHAN
Chairman of the Ave Maria Foundation,
Chairman of Legatus International, and
Chancellor of Ave Maria University.

MELISSA MOSCHELLA, PH.D.
Assistant Professor of Medical Ethics at
Columbia University.

GLORIA PURVIS
Host of *Morning Glory*, a daily morning
radio program broadcast from Washington D.C.
on EWTN Global Catholic Radio.

FATHER JOHN RICCARDO, STL, *Emeritus*
Priest of the Archdiocese of Detroit
and host of the daily radio program,
Christ is the Answer, broadcast on
EWTN Global Catholic Radio.

Episcopal Advisors to the Catholic Advisory Board:

HIS EMINENCE ADAM CARDINAL MAIDA
Archbishop Emeritus of Detroit

THE MOST REVEREND ALLEN VIGNERON
Archbishop of Detroit

NOTES

1   *Good Profit: How Creating Value for Others Built One of the World's Most Successful Companies*, Charles G. Koch, p. 251 (2015)

CHAPTER 12

IN MEMORIAM

Finally, brothers, whatever is true, whatever is honorable,
whatever is just, whatever is pure, whatever is lovely,
whatever is gracious, if there is any excellence and if there
is anything worthy of praise, think about these things.[1]
— ST. PAUL

I wish to pay particular tribute to three of the founding members of the Catholic Advisory Board: Bowie Kuhn, Phyllis Schlafly, and Michael Novak. They are giants, and I am honored to have worked with them. Even more, I am grateful to have known them as close friends. Their service to the Ave Maria Mutual Fund shareholders was enormous.

BOWIE KUHN
(1926 – 2007)

Without Bowie Kuhn and Tom Monaghan, Morally Responsible Investing and the Ave Maria Mutual Funds would not exist. This was their idea. They came to me seeking advice on how to implement the idea. Bowie once put it this way:

What seems to me to be possible is that... in achieving
the moral high ground, we might begin to change the
conduct of corporate America in some very critical
and important ways.

Bowie pondered problems, pursued solutions, and sought to resolve disputes. He looked on the bright side and tried to take into account the concerns of all parties.

As a faithful Catholic, he promoted public policy rooted in the dignity of every human being. Because he recognized that *to protect the innocent* is the foundational principle of justice, the plight of the unborn was particularly dear to him. He understood that by virtue of their state in life, the unborn are literally the most innocent and most vulnerable of all human beings.

Bowie dreamed big, welcomed people, and personified compassion. One of his primary commitments during the final years of his life was to visit HIV/AIDS patients in area hospitals. He listened to them, shared stories, and most importantly, accompanied them.

Of course, in so many ways, Bowie was larger than life. He had served as Commissioner of Major League Baseball for 15 years, and yet, for the rest of his life was known as the Commish. I recall walking with Bowie in New York City twenty years after he had retired. We had appointments to discuss the Ave Maria Mutual Funds with investment advisers and reporters. As we walked down the street, a gentleman shouted out with sincere and great enthusiasm, "Hey Commish, how ya doin'!" Bowie never tired of smiling and waving to his many admirers.

Bowie had a photographic memory, particularly concerning all things baseball. He could recall specific circumstances and precise details from countless games played decades earlier.

Bowie was a well-educated and refined man, earning his undergraduate degree in economics from Princeton and law degree from the University of Virginia. He governed over challenging times in major league baseball as it transitioned through racial issues, free agency, difficult negotiations between the Major League Players Association and the club owners, and a players' strike that lasted nearly two months. These posed major challenges to the tradition-laden national pastime.

Though he struggled with players and owners at times, he always sought to do what he believed was in the best interest of baseball. He is credited with Major League Baseball's remarkable growth, from twenty to twenty-six teams. More than forty-five and a half million fans attended a major league baseball game in 1983, the final year of his contract, though he remained in office one more year.[2]

Bowie served as the first Chairman of the Catholic Advisory Board, beginning in May 2001. He was instrumental in opening doors and recruiting other Board members. Everybody loved Bowie. I tagged along for the ride. On one occasion a Cardinal of the Catholic Church agreed to meet with us to learn about the Ave Maria Mutual Funds. At the last minute, Bowie was not able to attend the meeting. The Cardinal had a particularly tight schedule that day and agreed to speak with us in between appointment. When the Cardinal walked in to the designated room at the designated time, he seemed surprised and disappointed. He looked around, and then, said to me, "George, I hope you won't take this the wrong way. I'm happy to meet with you; but you see, I've never met Bowie and was so looking forward to this opportunity." That is the effect Bowie had on people. He was an approachable, generous, talented, thoughtful, and cheerful professional. He is greatly missed.

PHYLLIS SCHLAFLY
(1924 – 2016)

I have never met anyone quite like Phyllis Schlafly. She was a modern-day Joan of Arc. By this I mean nothing daunted her and she proceeded with grace and grit. Her accomplishments are staggering. Phyllis authored or edited 27 books, wrote a syndicated column that appeared in 100 newspapers, published a monthly newsletter for decades, hosted a weekly radio program, generated approximately 8,000 three-minute radio commentaries aired on 500 stations, appeared on all of the major networks, wrote and produced several documentaries, and founded Eagle Forum.[3]

She was a brilliant student. The valedictorian of her high school class, she graduated from Washington University in St. Louis early despite working 48 hours a week at an ammunition plant during the height of WWII. She then earned a master's degree from Harvard (Radcliffe), graduating just shy of her 21st birthday. She returned to Washington University in her fifties and earned a law degree. She also raised six children, teaching all of them to read before they began school. Her children went on to become accomplished professionals — three lawyers, one physician, one Ph.D. mathematician, and one business executive. She was married to her husband for 44 years who himself was an accomplished attorney. In 1992, a year before her husband passed away, she was named Illinois Mother of the Year.[4]

In 2008, just shy of her 84th birthday, she received an honorary degree from her alma mater. Prior to the ceremony, 14 members of the law faculty signed a letter protesting the University's decision. Though one of the law school's most accomplished graduates (and an inspiration to millions of men and women), the situation grew grimmer on the day of the ceremony. As this dignified widow crossed the stage, one-third of the graduating class and some of the faculty stood and turned their back.

Of all her achievements, Phyllis is perhaps best known for single handedly defeating the Equal Rights Amendment (ERA). When she began the *Stop ERA* campaign in 1972, the task seemed impossible. The House, Senate, and President Nixon had given their approval and now it was a matter of persuading 38 states to ratify the measure. This seemed inevitable particularly because the National Organization for Women (NOW) and 80 partner organizations were well organized to proceed. Within two years, 30 states ratified the ERA. Persuading eight more states within the remaining five-year timeline seemed likely. But such analysis underestimated the impact of Phyllis Schlafly.

As of the deadline, March 22, 1979, NOW had fallen short by 3 states. Additionally, four states had changed their minds and rescinded their support for the ERA. The National Organization for Women filed lawsuits challenging the states that had rescinded, and they requested an extension. Supporters on the Hill passed a bill granting an extension, and President Carter signed the bill, but even he questioned the legitimacy of the extension on procedural grounds. Ultimately, the U.S. Supreme Court ruled the matter moot three years later concluding that the ERA had failed to gain the necessary 38 states.

How did this happen? A glimpse of Mrs. Schlafly's impact occurred early in the process when in 1973, she agreed to debate Betty Friedan, a fiery and formidable foe. As President of the National Organization for Woman, Mrs. Friedan seemed invincible. But Mrs. Schlafly pointed out her concerns and her logic resonated. She argued that the ERA was not necessary in light of the passage of the Equal Pay Act of 1963 and the Civil Rights Act of 1964. She also noted that the ERA would harm women — women would be placed in combat; alimony and Social Security could be jeopardized; custody battles would be more intense; abortion would become a woman's right (What about the right of unborn girls?); same sex marriage would be a logical consequence; similarly, some would call for the elimination of single-sex bathrooms and locker rooms; and other impacts that would undermine the family. Phyllis got under Betty's skin. Betty blurted out that she would like to burn Phyllis at the stake.[5] Another parallel to St. Joan of Arc.

When Tom Monaghan approached Phyllis to ask whether she would serve on the Catholic Advisory Board, she accepted on the spot. She knew that anything Tom was involved with would be trustworthy. And she wanted to do whatever she could to stand for innocent human life and against Planned Parenthood, pornography, and all that undermines the family. One of her last books, *Who Killed The American Family?* analyzes the forces aligned against the family and points to solutions. A brief excerpt:

> When the famous French commentator Alexis de
> Tocqueville traveled the United States in the mid-
> nineteenth century, he recognized that respect for
> marriage is almost uniquely American. He wrote:
> 'There is certainly no country in the world where the
> tie of marriage is more respected than in America,
> or where conjugal happiness is more highly or
> worthily appreciated. While the European endeavors
> to forget his domestic troubles by agitating society,
> the American derives from his own home that love
> of order which he afterwards carries with him into
> public affairs.'
>
> It should be evident that the American nuclear
> family is a good thing, and laws, policies, and social
> conventions that undermine the family are bad things.
> All social statistics confirm that American-style
> marriage has been good for women, good for men,
> good for children, good for society, good for freedom,
> and good for our high standard of living. Real-life
> experience has given our lawmakers and judges a
> rational basis for concluding that marriage is a social
> good that should be protected and encouraged by laws
> and when challenged in the courts...

The Great Depression of the 1930s, when millions of men were unemployed, didn't kill the American family. World War II, when we sent 16 million men to fight on faraway battlefields, requiring long absences from home, didn't kill it. What happened in the 1970s, '80s, and '90s to break up the family structure that seemed so secure in the 1950s and '60s?

This book connects the dots to explain how those changes happened and who is responsible for killing the traditional family. There is no single cause. The American family was destroyed by a combination of political activists, judges, economic theorists, self-proclaimed experts, and left-wing politicians — with different motives that produced the same result.[6]

Phyllis published this book at age 90, two years before she passed away. As with Bowie and Michael, Phyllis understood that time is our most precious resource. She consistently sought to advance truth, goodness, and beauty. The Catholic Church teaches that God is truth, goodness, and beauty.[7] Phyllis served on the Catholic Advisory Board with distinction. I am grateful for her many contributions and honored to have counted her among my friends.

MICHAEL NOVAK
(1933 – 2017)

Michael Novak may be the humblest, most accomplished intellectual I have ever known. He was as proud of the neighborhood where he came from in Johnstown, Pennsylvania as having earned numerous degrees. His priorities were faith, family, and country. He had the courage to pursue the truth wherever it led and to change course. This is particularly difficult in politics. For several years, he had advised and written speeches for prominent Democrats, including 1972 Democratic Vice- Presidential candidate Sargent Shriver, running mate to Senator George McGovern. As time passed, he could not ignore the evidence that socialism failed everywhere it had been tried. The poor were always worse off.

Michael Novak was an original thinker. Whether popular or not, he articulated the truth that the evidence revealed. By transferring ownership of the means of production to the state, socialism poisons the culture — the family, the schools, the neighborhoods, the communities, and the workforce. Rather than the Great Seal's motto, *From Many One*, and the nation's motto, *In God We Trust*, socialism breeds a spirit of discontent, disrespect, and ultimately chaos. Socialism erodes incentive and destroys initiative.

While many Catholic intellectuals looked for a middle way between socialism and capitalism, Novak found a third way; a tri-partite approach in the form of a three in one, integrated system of liberty — political, economic, and moral. *The Spirit of Democratic Capitalism* (1982), his crowning achievement, presented this perspective. This is one of those rare works that literally changed the world. It played a key role in the peaceful demise of Soviet-style socialism in 1989. Underground publishers risked everything to distribute this work behind the Iron Curtain.

Leaders would be wise to keep a copy of *The Spirit of Democratic Capitalism* (1982) handy. Socialism appeals to the well-intended and to those who relish power — a dangerous mix. The powerful have a history of manipulating the well-intended. Near the end of his life, Novak describes his own awakening in his autobiography, *Writing from Left to Right: My Journey from Liberal to Conservative.* Here he eloquently describes socialism's fatal flaw:

> The most underreported fact of the twentieth century
> was the death of socialism as a plausible idea for the
> future. In practice, it did not work. More than that,
> socialism's underlying theories made it impossible for
> it to work. The best hope of the poor in the world was
> not socialism. The actual history of my own family
> and millions of other poor families showed Marxism
> to be the opiate of intellectuals and students. The
> much despised "capitalism," combined with a polity of
> law and rights and a culture of spirit, routinely turned
> workers into middle-class families, with positive
> attitudes toward personal initiative and personal
> responsibility.[8]

Three nations — the Czech Republic, Poland, and Slovakia —

awarded him their highest foreign civilian award. In 1994, he received the Templeton Prize for Progress in Religion. He worked for several U.S. presidents and served on the boards of Radio Free Europe and Radio Liberty for eleven years. He taught at several select institutions including Harvard, Stanford, and Notre Dame. He received twenty-seven honorary degrees, including four in Latin America. He wrote more than 50 books on a wide range of topics from sports to the Founding Fathers weaving universal truths, keen observations, wonderful stories, and philosophical principles throughout. [9]

Michael Novak knew prominent figures throughout the world, but he was most honored that Pope Saint John Paul welcomed him as his friend. Michael was immediately captivated by the vibrant 58 year-old Karol Wojtyla when he was announced to the world as Pope John Paul II in October 1978. The first non-Italian pope in four hundred years and hailing from behind the Iron Curtain — clearly history in the making. Michael's grandparents emigrated from rural Slovakia, not far from where Pope Saint John Paul grew up. Michael swelled with joy and pride. [10]

Pope Saint John Paul and Michael Novak met for the first time in 1991. While attending a conference near Florence, Michael traveled to Rome to visit the U.S. Ambassador to the Vatican. During dinner, a phone call drew him away. When he returned, he explained that he had just been invited to dinner with Pope John Paul II the following evening. The Pope had recently released *Centesimus Annus*, an encyclical commemorating the 100th anniversary of *Rerum Novarum*, the foundational document concerning the Church's teaching on capital and labor. Paragraph 42 of *Centesimus Annus* favorably discusses the central principle from

The Spirit of Democratic Capitalism. [11]

Pope Saint John Paul and Michael Novak remained close friends for the next 14 years. By way of illustration, Pope Saint John Paul told his biographer, George Weigel: "Michael Novak says he is Slovak. But he is actually Polish."[12] Upon hearing this, Michael wrote the Pope, "By the Magisterium I may be Polish, but by family, genetics, and geography, I am Slovak." Just a few weeks later, Michael discovered a map on the inner wall of an ancient castle. The map demonstrated that the region where Michael's ancestors are from was part of Poland for three centuries. Michael wrote a follow up letter to the Pope: "Darn infallibility! You are right again, and I was wrong."[13]

Near the end of his life, Michael had an appointment as a visiting professor at Ave Maria University. I asked him what he would be teaching. He replied, "Anything they ask me to teach." He wasn't boasting. He had reached a point in his profession that he literally could teach anything. This was fact. He was a man of letters and a guardian of truth. We greatly benefited from his counsel and support. His work will endure because truth is timeless.

FAREWELL

Through their words, their reputations, and their heroic witness, Bowie Kuhn, Phyllis Schlafly, and Michael Novak will be remembered forever. They played vitally important public roles. I am eternally grateful that they also dedicated their wisdom and expertise in support of the Ave Maria Mutual Funds. As with St. Paul, they can safely say: "I have competed well; I have finished the race; I have kept the faith."[14] May they rest in peace.

NOTES

1   *Philippians*, 4:8-9; www.usccb.org/bible/scripture.cfm?bk=58&ch=004&v=003

2   http://www.baseball-almanac.com/articles/bowie_kuhn_biography.shtml

3   http://eagleforum.org/about/bio.html

4   https://en.wikipedia.org/wiki/Phyllis_Schlafly

5   https://www.washingtonpost.com/national/phyllis-schlafly-a-conservative-activist-has-died-at-age-92/2016/09/05/513420e2-73bc-11e6-be4f-3f42f2e5a49e_story.html?utm_term=.0b1283e5e06d

6   *Who Killed the American Family?* Phyllis Schlafly, 1-3 (2014)

7   https://en.wikipedia.org/wiki/Transcendentals

8   *Writing from Left to Right: My Journey from Liberal to Conservative*, Michael Novak, 300 (2013)

9   https://en.wikipedia.org/wiki/Michael_Novak

10   *Writing from Left to Right: My Journey from Liberal to Conservative*, Michael Novak, 10-11 (2013)

11   https://www.michaelnovak.net/bio/

12   *Writing from Left to Right: My Journey from Liberal to Conservative*, Michael Novak, 302 (2013)

13   *Writing from Left to Right: My Journey from Liberal to Conservative*, Michael Novak, 302-303 (2013)

14   2 Timothy 4:7-8; www.usccb.org/bible/2timothy/4

CHAPTER 13

THE BEST WAY
FORWARD

A nation's moral life is the foundation of its culture.[1]

— JUDGE ROBERT BORK

In these pages, I have addressed the desire to pursue capital market gains in a way that builds up culture and does not compromise conscience. The timeless truths articulated in the Declaration of Independence are also imprinted on every human heart (i.e., the natural law). We are endowed with certain unalienable rights (i.e., rights that exist because we exist), including the right to life, liberty, and the pursuit of happiness (i.e., private property). Because these truths reflect the dignity of the human being made in the image and likeness of God, they are foundational to all healthy, thriving, and prosperous societies.

Morally Responsible Investing enables investing consistent with these truths. The business community *can* be influenced. It is responsive to a force other than politics – *money*. By investing in businesses that do not fund or in any manner support pornography, abortion, or Planned Parenthood, investors encourage businesses to support marriage, family, and the culture.

Ave Maria Mutual Funds' success is due in large part to its philosophy – one that puts equal weight on investment performance and pro-life, pro-family values. Since its inception in 2001, Ave Maria Mutual Funds have seen tremendous growth. Today, assets under management exceed $2 billion dollars, in five different mutual funds, with five different investment objectives, all composed of trust quality stocks and bonds.

Investing in morally responsible mutual funds has become increasingly popular as more and more Americans seek to align their portfolios with their convictions. While it is essential that the portfolio companies do not violate core teachings of the Roman Catholic Church, Ave Maria Mutual Funds appeal to a broad range of faith traditions because the core teachings of the Catholic Church align with universal truths, particularly as expressed through our nation's founding principles. G.K. Chesterton was right. America was founded on a creed,[2] and a century ago, Congress adopted the following expression of that creed:

> I believe in the United States of America, as a
> government of the people, by the people, for the
> people; whose just powers are derived from the consent
> of the governed; a democracy in a republic; a sovereign
> Nation of many sovereign States; a perfect union, one
> and inseparable; established upon those principles of
> freedom, equality, justice, and humanity for which
> American patriots sacrificed their lives and fortunes.

> I therefore believe it is my duty to my country to love
> it, to support its Constitution, to obey its laws, to

respect its flag, and to defend it against all enemies.

—WILLIAM TYLER PAGE, THE AMERICAN'S CREED[3]

The American Creed succinctly states the core structures and principles that facilitate success in the United States. Michael Novak's "three systems in one" (i.e., market economy, a government respectful of rights, and cultural institutions) cogently considers this context. We are a nation grounded in timeless truths. Truth promotes freedom. *The Spirit of Democratic Capitalism* is the spirit of freedom.

MARKET ECONOMY

Just as hundreds of years ago the free enterprise system inspired entrepreneurs in the Netherlands and England to invest in the Mayflower, the free enterprise system today continues to provide the risk/reward conditions that inspire greatness. With the prospect of being rewarded for excellence, a market economy incentivizes the production of quality products, optimal services, and reasonable prices. Competition promotes quality. To win market share, people must think creatively, seek solutions collaboratively, and proceed courageously.

Rules and procedures exist to foster fair practices and equal opportunity. Bureaucrats who participate in the rulemaking process are not directly accountable to the people. If these individuals fail to proceed in a politically neutral manner, they jeopardize the system. To guard against this, a mechanism has been in place since 1816 through the U.S. House of Representatives – the Committee on Oversight and Government Reform.[4]

A market economy inspires ingenuity, encourages *integral human development*,[5] and provides a high standard of living for the greatest number of people (particularly as reflected in basic services and environmental quality – clean air, water, and soil). Human flourishing begins with respect for the dignity of every human being and grows through *charity in truth*.[6] A market economy – supported by sound government structures and generous cultural institutions – empowers communities, strengthens a nation's moral life, and provides the foundation for its culture.

A GOVERNMENT RESPECTFUL OF RIGHTS

In 1831, after traveling throughout America, historian and political scientist Alexis de Tocqueville found much to be admired – committed marriages, strong families, and vibrant communities.[7] He used the French expression *laissez-faire* ("let do") to indicate that, by and large, commerce flows efficiently in the United States.[8] A government respectful of rights creates a favorable climate for commerce. The U.S. Constitution makes clear the roles and responsibilities of the three branches of government: legislative (Article 1); executive (Article 2); and judicial (Article 3). This contributes to creating a stable environment for commercial activity.

The Constitution includes two mechanisms that help keep the federal government in check. First, separation of powers (i.e., three branches of government); and second, sharing of powers (i.e., among the federal, state, and local governments). The federal judiciary has proven to be the branch of government least willing to operate within the scope of authority granted to it under the Constitution. This has long been a concern. In his *First Inaugural Address*, President Lincoln said:

[T]he candid citizen must confess that if the policy
of the Government upon vital questions affecting the
whole people is to be irrevocably fixed by decisions of
the Supreme Court...

the people will have ceased to be their own rulers,
having to that extent practically resigned their
Government into the hands of that eminent tribunal.[9]

The U.S. Supreme Court's failure to limit their decisions to the text of the Constitution has disrupted the separation of powers. This poses a grave threat. Judge Bork put it this way in his 1996 New York Times bestseller, *Slouching Towards Gomorrah: Modern Liberalism and American Decline*:

The judicial adoption of the tenets of modern liberalism
has produced a crisis of legitimacy. Contrary to the
plan of the American government, the Supreme
Court has usurped the powers of the people and their
elected representatives. We are no longer free to make
our own fundamental moral and cultural decisions
because the Court oversees all such matters, when and
as it chooses. The crisis of legitimacy occurs because
the political nation has no way of responding. The
Founders built into our government a system of checks
and balances, carefully giving to the national legislature
and the executive powers to check each other so as

to avoid either executive or legislative tyranny. The
Founders had no idea that a Court armed with a
written Constitution and the power of judicial review
could become not only the supreme legislature of the
land but a legislature beyond the reach of the ballot
box. Thinking of the Court as a minor institution,
they provided no safeguards against its assumption
of powers not legitimately its own and its consistent
abuse of those powers. Congress and the President
check and balance one another, but neither of them
can stop the Court's adventures in making and
enforcing left-wing policy.[10]

In *The Tempting of America*, written six years before *Slouching Towards Gomorrah*, Judge Bork explained that judges are tempted to go beyond their role defined by the Constitution:

In law, the moment of temptation is the moment of
choice, when a judge realizes that in the case before
him his strongly held view of justice, his political
and moral imperative, is not embodied in a statute or
in any provision of the Constitution. He must then
choose between his version of justice and abiding
by the American form of government. Yet the desire
to do justice, whose nature seems to him obvious,
is compelling, while the concept of constitutional
process is abstract, rather arid, and the abstinence it

counsels unsatisfying. To give in to temptation, this
one time, solves an urgent human problem, and a faint
crack appears in the American foundation. A judge has
begun to rule where a legislator should.[11]

The Supreme Court's decision in *Griswold* created a right not contained within the text of the Constitution.[12] This new right, known as the right to privacy, became the basis for legalizing abortion. In the area of pornography, a key U.S. Supreme Court decision, *Jacobellis*, reversed an Ohio Supreme Court decision that had ruled a film was not protected by the First Amendment. The U.S. Supreme Court reversed, but offered no clear rationale. There are nine Justices on the U.S. Supreme Court. *Jacobellis* produced seven opinions: the plurality, four concurring, and two dissenting. None had the support of more than two justices. Justice Potter Stewart's concurring opinion reveals the difficulty:

I shall not today attempt further to define the kinds
of material I understand to be embraced within that
shorthand description (i.e., "hard-core pornography");
and perhaps I could never succeed in intelligibly doing
so. But I know it when I see it, and the motion picture
involved in this case is not that.[13]

Justice Stewart's candor is instructive. His opinion has been criticized as lacking legal analysis, but isn't it possible that the paucity of analysis results from the absence of a true Constitutional basis for protecting pornography as free speech?

At the heart of the matter stands the question of whether pornography constitutes free speech. Did the drafters of the First Amendment intend *freedom of speech* to include commercializing, monetizing, and exploiting images that undermine the dignity of the human person? One thing is very clear. Pornography is not harmless; it is a serious and growing public health threat. Morally Responsible Investing provides a positive retort and hopefully will be part of an awakening that raises community standards and ends the scourge of pornography.

"We the People" is articulated in the Preamble to the U.S. Constitution. Are we to be governed through the separation of powers amid three branches of government with a division of responsibilities between the federal, state, and local governments? Or will the federal government continue to balloon in size and bureaucracy, unleashed from checks and balances and steeped in socialism rather than limited government? This is the fundamental divide between conservatives (limited government) and liberals (socialism). For investors and the good of the economy, history makes clear that socialism never works. Only a republican form (i.e., powers vested in the people exercised through representatives) of limited government can achieve what Michael Novak means by *a government respectful of rights*.

CULTURAL INSTITUTIONS

The third of the three parts set forth by Michael Novak in the *Spirit of Democratic Capitalism* consists of supporting cultural institutions. Of these, none is more important than the family. In her book *Who Killed the American Family?*, Phyllis Schlafly included the following excerpt from the 2012 Republican Party Platform:

The institution of marriage is the foundation of civil
society. Its success as an institution will determine
our success as a nation. It has been proven by both
experience and endless social science studies that
traditional marriage is best for children...

The success of marriage directly impacts the economic
well-being of individuals. Furthermore, the future of
marriage affects freedom. The lack of family formation
not only leads to more government costs, but also to
more government control over the lives of its citizens
in all aspects.[14]

Strong families contribute to a strong economy. The economy also
benefits from a culture rooted in virtue and supported by formative
institutions steeped in respect for the dignity of the human person.
These institutions include our churches, synagogues, schools, hospitals, charities, community organizations, chambers of commerce, and
other networks that pledge allegiance to the United States and seek
the common good.

Beyond the family, our schools play a prominent role in forming
cultural attitudes. Depending on what is taught and how, schools can
build up or tear down culture. Significantly, schools shape the world-
views of those who eventually serve in government. Lincoln put it this
way: "The philosophy of the school room in one generation will be the
philosophy of government in the next."[15] Do our schools adequately
teach the natural law principles that undergird our nation?

Upon Lincoln's death, the Russian novelist, Leo Tolstoy, described Lincoln as "A Christ in miniature."[16] In and through Christ rests eternal law, the ultimate standard for determining whether a law is just. Just laws are essential to the pursuit of happiness, and the natural law tradition provides the surest way to achieve and sustain a just legal system.

A profound appreciation for the natural law inspired and animated Rev. Martin Luther King, Jr.'s work. By way of illustration, in his *Letter from Birmingham Jail*, Dr. King cites St. Augustine for the proposition that "an unjust law is no law at all." To determine whether a law is just, Dr. King presents an explanation by St. Thomas Aquinas: "An unjust law is a human law that is not rooted in eternal law and natural law." King goes on to write: "Any law that uplifts human personality is just. Any law that degrades human personality is unjust."

As was the case in segregation and slavery, abortion and pornography profoundly "degrade human personality." President Lincoln and Dr. King relied upon the timeless truths in our nation's founding documents to eliminate the injustice of slavery and segregation. They understood that our nation's natural law foundation is essential to ensuring liberty and justice for all. Will these same principles bring an end to abortion and pornography?[17]

Tom Monaghan and Bowie Kuhn were entirely right when they insisted, back at the start of the Ave Maria Mutual Funds, that a group of like-minded, motivated investors can make a difference, acting together with dedication and perseverance. And as our popes and serious Catholic scholars such as George Weigel, Robert George, Phyllis Schlafly, and Michael Novak have demonstrated, a climate of moral consistency is as important to business success as it is to the wellbeing of society in general.

Over the past two decades, we have demonstrated that an investment program operated within constraints determined by the concept of Morally Responsible Investing can show an excellent return. Our funds have performed well in up-markets and suffered less in down-markets. It has been my experience that there is a relationship between ethics and business results. Over time, those companies that are well managed tend to be the most successful, and morality is a vital component of good management.

This view is not completely impervious to quibbling, but it has a pedigree reaching all the way back through Adam Smith (who linked such moral virtues as prudence, justice, industry, frugality and constancy with the satisfaction of self-interest), through the rabbinic sages (who waxed poetic on commercial ethics in page after page of the Talmud), to the Golden Rule and its firm foundation, the Ten Commandments.

Pope Emeritus Benedict XVI weighed in strongly on this point in a paper he delivered at a 1985 symposium in Rome. Then-Cardinal Ratzinger stated that "market rules function only when a moral consensus exists and sustains them." He observed that a woeful secularist tradition has fostered the specious idea that, even if they have faith, people in business should "regard their Christianity as a private concern, while as members of the business community they abide by the laws of the economy." He rejected this false dichotomy, declaring prophetically:

> It is becoming an increasingly obvious fact of
> economic history that the development of economic
> systems which concentrate on the common good
> depends on a determinate ethical system, which

in turn can be born and sustained only by strong religious convictions. Conversely, it has also become obvious that the decline of such discipline can actually cause the laws of the market to collapse. An economic policy that is ordered not only to the good of the group — indeed, not only to the common good of a determinate state — but to the common good of the family of man demands a maximum of ethical discipline and thus a maximum of religious strength.[18]

President Lincoln expressed a similar sentiment:

"The only assurance of our nation's safety is to lay our foundation in morality and religion."[19]

Economic systems, government structures, and cultural institutions ordered to the common good and secured through just laws provide the optimal context for human flourishing.

THE LONG VIEW

Given the turmoil that's engulfed our economy, this may seem like an odd time to bring out an investment book. The confidence required to put hard-earned money into the securities of companies so shaken in recent months has surely been tested. And at the time these words are written, it looks like there are more tests ahead with the threat of a trade war with China, North Korea's nuclear ambitions, and Iran's support for terrorism. President Trump and his team have their hands full. The markets are nervous (they always are).

And yet, witnessing so much money evaporate so quickly, from a Value Investing perspective, this is a uniquely propitious moment. Stock prices have been grossly distorted by factors that do not reflect the actual strength and resilience of American industry.

This simple fact remains: For most people, the stock market is the most efficient vehicle for creating wealth. Back in 1991, my colleague, Richard L. Platte, Jr. CFA, who serves as our President and Chief Investment Officer, wrote a market commentary on investment prospects in an economy battered by recession and the first Gulf War; he updated it in 2001, after the "dot-com bust." In it, he noted the swings in investor attitudes, from wild euphoria to abject fear, which had left investors in similar states of shellshock at both points in market history. Rick's observations remain pertinent to this day:

> The question would seem to be, on which of these
> two diametrically opposing views of the market
> [optimism or pessimism] should investors be
> basing their investment decisions? Neither, in our
> estimation. Why? Because they both represent a
> very fickle popular sentiment, and are the product
> of a very temporary view of the economy and equity
> market. It is our contention that investors should
> focus on the long-term perspective, and if they do,
> they will be drawn to significant ownership of
> high-quality common stocks.

When one takes a short-term view of either the economy or the stock market, it is easy to be alternately immobilized and stampeded by changing market psychology and momentary impressions of the economic environment. The often-overlooked facet of this phenomenon is that the market discounts the consensus view, be it positive or negative. So if investors are, in the aggregate, frightened by prospects for the economy, stock prices move lower to reflect that view. Conversely, when optimism reigns, high stock prices reflect that, too.

Taking the longer-term perspective has the effect of smoothing out many of the bumps and eliminating much of the noise one is subjected to when attempting to make decisions based upon short-term views. There is risk in stocks. They go up, and they go down. But, over the long term, the financial significance of recessions and even wars is vastly diminished, as the predominant trend for stock prices is up.

Rick provided a small chart that demonstrated the comparative returns on $1.00 invested in various asset classes, showing what each investment would have been worth relative to the average rate of inflation since 1926. The figures are quite striking.

Here the comparisons are extended to the end of 2017:

COMPARATIVE INVESTMENT RETURNS[20]

	AMOUNT INVESTED IN 1926	MARKET VALUE IN 2017	COMPOUND ANNUAL RETURN 1926–2017
Common Stocks	$1.00	$7,353	10.2%
Long-term Treasury Bonds	$1.00	$143	5.5%
Treasury Bills	$1.00	$21	3.4%
Rate of Inflation	$1.00	$14	2.9%

The chart makes it abundantly clear: Even allowing for the 2008 market debacle and every other recession that has occurred in more than nine decades of market tracking (including the crash of 1929), equities are far and away the most productive type of investment over time. And that holds true whether you invest in individual stocks or mutual funds. Through price appreciation and dividends, stocks have produced long term total returns of 10% per year.

Jeremy Siegel, from the University of Pennsylvania's Wharton School, makes the same point in his bestselling investment book, *Stocks for the Long Run*:

> The long-term perspective radically changes one's view
> of the risk of stocks. The short-term fluctuations in the
> stock market, which loom so large to investors when
> they occur, are insignificant when compared to the
> upward movement of equity values over time.[21]

I've long contended that market corrections are buying opportunities. At the depths of the 2008-09 downturn, when capital had fled the markets in a massive liquidation of equities worse than anything I'd ever seen in five decades of investment counsel, the inevitability of recovery was apparent. Some $4 trillion of investor cash was sitting in money market funds as shelter against further loss, the highest cash-to-equity relationship on record. You might think that's a sign of utter doom: 40 percent of market capitalization cringing in fear of total destruction to come. But it's really the fuel for a future bull market. Such a mountain of liquidity cannot sit squirreled away indefinitely, because money can't be idle forever. Investors ultimately seek opportunities to make their cash productive, and that need will always take them back to the stock market.

Here in 2018, many people invest looking backward instead of forward. Even if there are more bumps and slides ahead, in the words of my colleague, Rick Platte, "the predominant trend for stock prices is up."

FAITH & FAMILY

While market performance and investment potential are critical considerations, the particular focus of this book is faith. In these pages I have addressed the desire to pursue capital market gains in a way that does not compromise conscience. Moreover, I've called for a great movement of investors who are motivated by religious commitment to act in concert, exerting pressure on the business community for the sake of positive moral change. And this may be the best of all times to be promoting such a movement.

Despite the distinctively Catholic name, the Ave Maria Mutual

Funds have never been sectarian. We have always sought to reach across denominational lines, and the opportunity currently before us provides encouragement to redouble our efforts to attract non-Catholic investors. In this way we can reinforce the interfaith unity of the pro-life movement. What could be better than mutual economic interest to cement relationships between people who share common faith and a set of values so much more fundamental than the points of doctrine on which they differ? Our common commitment, after all, is to God and to His most precious gift: life. Morally Responsible Investing is a tool with which we can serve Him together.

The dearly departed Catholic Advisory Board member, Phyllis Schlafly, wrote and spoke extensively about family breakdown, which she noted is intimately connected with a general decline of spirituality throughout our culture and a disheartening breakdown in moral standards and civil behavior. Phyllis points to the collapse of discipline in schools, rising crime rates, increases in poverty, all of which correlate with the destruction of families.

For my part, I think a restoration of "family values" (that most overworked of clichés, but nonetheless a phrase that captures a real and persistent human longing) would be a tremendous encouragement both to the pro-life movement and to Morally Responsible Investing. Investors — Catholics and Protestants alike — may well be more inclined to add a moral component to their portfolios. Under such conditions, the effort I seek to mount in defense of life becomes ever more plausible. In a turn on one of the more cynical sound bites to emerge during the early days of the Obama regime, it would be a matter of "not letting a good crisis go to waste."

The business community *can* be influenced, because it is responsive to a force other than politics — that is, to *money*. Certainly, corporations have been buffeted by any number of ideological fads. Those of us who lived through the great era of "sensitivity training" can attest to the impact of politics on business. And it's clear enough that most of the current emphasis on the "greening" of corporations is not only irrelevant to the actual concerns of businesses, it actually runs counter to plain economic sense.

For all of that, the ongoing requirement of profit makes companies much less willing to jump through the flaming hoops of intellectual whim than, say, public agencies or academic institutions. It also makes them more responsive to the native practicality of those ordinary folks from whom their profits (and capital) come. Business does have a dog in the morality fight, because business stands on culture, and the basis of culture is religion ("cult"). As David P. Goldman, the Asia Times' commentator who styles himself "Spengler," has noted, those cultures in which people exhibit the optimism made possible by spiritual confidence — America foremost among them — are still experiencing both population growth and economic expansion. It is Christianity, with its insistence on the transformative power of faith and individual moral responsibility that makes such confidence possible. Those cultures that have lost spiritual vitality through the decline of faith, or where religion binds people to tribal patterns and social norms that deny the inherent dignity of individual life, stand on the brink of economic collapse.

Religiously motivated investors thus have a strong case to make, and we must not shrink from making it. While it might take organized effort to accomplish our goal, the moral cause in which we seek to enlist

American business is clearly for business' benefit.

This is our moment. The strong condition of the economy has given investors of conscience a chance not only to avoid stocks tainted by moral ambiguity, but also to become a significant presence on the American financial scene through strategic joint action. And not just Catholics, by any means. It's already happening. I estimate that about five percent of our 100,000 shareholders are non-Catholics, and we receive inquiries from more such folks all the time — though there is often an air of hesitancy about those contacts. I remember getting a call from a Protestant minister in the early days of the Ave Maria Mutual Funds. He asked me very sheepishly, "Do you have to be Catholic to invest in your fund?"

"Of course not," I replied. "We don't discriminate against anybody."

"Oh, thank God," he said. "One of my clergy colleagues and I want to invest in your fund because we're strongly pro-life. Your funds are the only funds I know of that have such a strong pro-life stance. Send us a prospectus and application. We'll put a check in the mail to you immediately."

Abortion was a big issue in the last election and polls tell us that there was a significant percentage of voters who saw it as a key concern, specifically those people who attend church regularly, are active in their faith communities, and hold traditional moral views. That's our constituency. I'm convinced the investors are out there, enough to build a movement that can eventually achieve a critical mass.

This is no quixotic crusade. What I know we *can* do is identify companies that have both good investment merits and policies that are consistent with Morally Responsible Investment principles, and then become owners of those companies. In this way we will become an important shareholder bloc whose contentment corporate managers will recognize is in their best interest to ensure. Influencing corporate behavior is possible. Anti-abortion activist, Tom Strobhar, president of the Dayton, Ohio-based investment firm, Pro-Vita Advisors, has succeeded in persuading American Express and several other major companies to stop donating to Planned Parenthood. I was present when he confronted Warren Buffett, one of the most successful investors of all time. Taking the microphone at a Berkshire Hathaway annual meeting in front of 22,000 shareholders, Tom challenged Warren Buffett's support for abortion. I admire Tom's courageous and articulate stand for life.

I have had many conversations with corporate managers about the moral implications of their companies' policies and practices. Some executives simply don't care, but more than once I have seen my words elicit genuine surprise. The negative societal effects of what their companies do sometimes just haven't occurred to them. We strive to help good-hearted and open-minded people see the connections.

In any event, we can gain influence by being practical investors. And as we increase in numbers and extend our influence to more and more companies, we will — like the mustard seed that, in the parable, grew to enormous size — achieve greater presence and stronger impact over a wider area. Today we are having a positive effect on society, because we are influencing business in a positive way.

It is my hope that through this book you have gained a perspective on Morally Responsible Investing, what it is, and why it works. It is my further hope that the reader has gained a renewed respect for our system of limited government responsible to the people as ingeniously set forth in the United States Constitution and animated by the Declaration of Independence. Investments require a free enterprise system and a free enterprise system can only thrive in the context of democratic capitalism rooted in eternal principles of justice and overseen by a government with checks and balances and a society steeped in virtue.

May we always be a nation that embraces the melting pot notion of *From Many One* and forever recognizes that our rights reflect our eternal destination as beings made in the image and likeness of God. May we always proclaim *In God We Trust* and wholeheartedly pledge that we are *One Nation Under God*. And may you experience investment success with the peace of mind found in Morally Responsible Investing.

NOTES

1 *Slouching Towards Gomorrah: Modern Liberalism and American Decline*, Robert H. Bork (1996); *Slouching Towards Gomorrah, An Executive Summary*, Dr. Joseph B. Fuiten; https://www.cedarpark.org/wp-content/uploads/2013/10/gomorrah.pdf

2 https://www.goodreads.com/quotes/262437-america-is-the-only-nation-in-the-world-that-is; https://www.chesterton.org/america/

3 https://en.wikipedia.org/wiki/American_Creed

4 https://en.m.wikipedia.org/wiki/United_States_House_Committee_on_Oversight_and_Government_Reform

5 *Caritas in Veritate, On Integral Human Development In Charity and Truth*, Pope Benedict XVI, (2009)

6 *Caritas in Veritate, On Integral Human Development In Charity and Truth*, Pope Benedict XVI, (2009)

7 https://en.wikipedia.org/wiki/American_exceptionalism

8 https://en.wikipedia.org/wiki/Laissez-faire

9 *First Inaugural Address*, Abraham Lincoln (1861)

10 *Slouching Towards Gomorrah: Modern Liberalism and American Decline*, Robert H. Bork (1996); *Slouching Towards Gomorrah, An Executive Summary*, Dr. Joseph B. Fuiten; https://www.cedarpark.org/wp-content/uploads/2013/10/gomorrah.pdf

11 *The Tempting of America*, Robert H. Bork (1990)

12 *Griswold v. Connecticut*, 381 U.S. 479 (1965)

13 https://en.wikipedia.org/wiki/Jacobellis_v._Ohio

14 *Who Killed The American Family?*, Phyllis Schlafly, at 48 (2012)

15 *America's God and Country, Encyclopedia of Quotations*, William Federer at 392 (2000)

16 *America's God and Country, Encyclopedia of Quotations*, William Federer at 392 (2000)

17 https://en.wikipedia.org/wiki/Letter_from_Birmingham_Jail

18 *Market Economy and Ethics*, Joseph Cardinal Ratzinger (1985), available online from The Acton Institute http://www.acton.org/publications/occasionalpapers/publicat_occasionalpapers_ratzinger.php?view=print

19 *America's God and Country, Encyclopedia of Quotations*, William Federer at 392 (2000)

20 Source: Ibbotson Associates, a subsidiary of Morningstar.

21 *Stocks for the Long Run* by Jeremy J. Siegel, The McGraw Hill Companies, 2007.

IN GOD WE TRUST
by Michael Novak

SUNDAY, APRIL 30, 2000

How long are we going to keep this experiment, this America? We are "testing whether this nation can long endure," Lincoln said at Gettysburg. We're still testing. Does the new century mark our last? Is America a meteor that blazed across the heavens and is now exhausted? Or rather is our present moral fog a transient time of trial, those hours cold and dark before the ramparts' new gleaming? Are we near our end or at a beginning?

In answer to these questions, I want to do something relatively rare these days. I want to give a sense of the religious *energy* behind the American founding. For a hundred years scholars have stressed the role of the Enlightenment and John Locke in particular. But there are also first principles that come to us from Judaism and Christianity, especially from Judaism. The religious principles in the founding were and are important to many citizens, and they are probably indispensable to the moral health of the Republic, as Washington taught us in his Farewell Address: "Of all the dispositions and indispensable supports." Washington said "indispensable." Reason and faith are the two wings by which the American eagle took flight.

A COMMON FAITH

When our founders talked religiously about politics they borrowed mostly from the Jewish Testament, not the Christian. Scholars often mistakenly refer to the God of the founders as a deist god. But the founders talked about God in terms that are radically Jewish: Creator, Judge, and Providence. These were the names they most commonly used for him, notably in the Declaration of Independence. For the most part, these are not names that could have come from the Greeks or Romans but only from the Jewish Testament. Perhaps the founders avoided Christian language to avert divisiveness, since different colonies were founded under different Christian inspirations. All found common language in the language of the Jewish Testament.

Religious principles appear to be indispensable to the health of the Republic. Reason and faith are the two wings by which the American eagle took flight.

If I stress the religious elements of the story, it is because for the past century scholars have paid too much attention to Jefferson in these matters and ignored the other top one hundred founders, most of whom were profoundly religious men. The crucial point is that *all* the Founding Fathers — Jefferson included — shared in common a belief that a people cannot maintain liberty without religion. They understood the power of religion to their cause yet worried that in the eyes of God they would be found wanting. Here is John Adams in 1776:

"I sometimes tremble to think that although we are engaged in the best cause that ever employed the human heart, yet the prospect of success is doubtful, not for want of power or of wisdom but of virtue."

The founding generation had no munitions factory this side of the ocean, and yet they were facing the most powerful army and the largest navy in the world.

Besides, their unity was fragile. The people of Virginia did not like the people of Massachusetts. The people of Massachusetts did not think highly of the people of Georgia. If they were to stick together with people they didn't particularly like, the Americans needed virtues of tolerance, civic spirit, and a love of the common good.

Further, because the new nation couldn't compete in armed power, the colonists depended on high moral qualities in their leaders and on devotion in the people. In order to win, for instance, Washington had to avoid frontal combat and to rely on the moral endurance of his countrymen year after year. To this end, Washington issued an order that any soldier who used profane language would be drummed out of the army. He impressed upon his men that they were fighting for a cause that demanded a special moral appeal, and he wanted no citizen to be shocked by the language and behavior of his troops. The men had to show day by day that they fought under a special moral covenant.

FOUNDED IN PRAYER

In the first days of September 1774, from every region, members of the First Continental Congress were riding dustily toward Philadelphia, where they hoped to remind King George III of the rights due to them as Englishmen. As these delegates were gathering, news arrived that the king's troops were shelling Charlestown and Boston, and rumors flew that the city was being sacked, robbery and murder being committed. Those rumors later turned out not to be true, but that's the news they heard. Thus, as they gathered, the delegates were confronted with impending war. No wonder their first act as a Continental Congress was to request a session of prayer.

The crucial point is that all the Founding Fathers —
Jefferson included — shared in common a belief that
a people cannot maintain liberty without religion.

Mr. Jay of New York and Mr. Rutledge of South Carolina immediately spoke against this motion because (they said) Americans are so divided in religious sentiments — some Episcopalians, some Quakers, some Anabaptists, some Presbyterians, and some Congregationalists — that all could not join in the same act of prayer. Sam Adams rose to say that he could hear a prayer from any gentleman of piety and virtue, as long as he was a patriot. Adams moved that a Reverend Duché be asked to read prayers before Congress on the next morning. The motion carried.

Thus it happened that the first act of Congress on September 7, 1774, was an official prayer, pronounced by an Episcopalian clergyman dressed in his pontificals. And what did he read? He read a Jewish prayer, Psalm 35 in *The Book of Common Prayer*:

Plead my cause, O Lord, with them that strive with me.
Fight against them that fight against me. Take hold of
buckler and shield, and rise up for my help. Say to my
soul, "I am your salvation." Let those be ashamed and
dishonored who seek my life. Let those be turned back
and humiliated who devise evil against me.

Before the Reverend Duché knelt Washington, Henry, Randolph, Rutledge, Lee, and Jay. By their side, heads bowed, were the Puritan patriots, who could imagine at that moment their own homes being bombarded by the fleet or overrun by the king's troops. Over these bowed heads the Reverend Duché uttered what all testified was an eloquent prayer for America, for Congress, for the province of Massachusetts Bay, and especially for the town of Boston. The emotion in the room was palpable, and John Adams wrote to Abigail that night that he had never heard a better prayer or one so well pronounced:

"I never saw a greater effect upon an audience. It
seemed as if heaven had ordained that that Psalm be
read on that morning. It was enough to melt a stone.
I saw tears gush into the eyes of the old, grave pacific
Quakers of Philadelphia."

In this fashion, right at its beginning, this nation formed a covenant with God that is repeated in the Declaration: "with a firm reliance on the protection of Divine Providence." The founders pledged their fidelity to the will of God and asked God to protect their liberty. They would continue to enact this covenant in the years to come in many later acts of Congress.

A GOD OF ACTION

On the night before the battle of Long Island, the Americans received intelligence that the British were attacking the next morning and that Washington would be trapped with his whole army. Washington saw that there was only one way out — by boat. During the night, the Americans gathered as many boats as they could. There weren't enough. Morning came, and more than half the troops were still on shore. A huge fog rolled in and covered them until noon. They escaped, and when the British closed the trap, there was no one there. The Americans interpreted that fog as an act of Providence.

In the preaching of the time, Americans learned as follows: Providence does not mean that God works magically. Rather, from all time every detail of the tapestry is known to the one who weaves it. To the Eternal God, there is neither time nor sequence, but every detail of the tapestry is visible to him as if in one simultaneous moment, each thing acting independently and freely but cohering as a whole. Thus, the rival general on the morning of the great battle comes down with dysentery and can't concentrate. Such events were construed as God's will — not circumstance or chance. In the Jewish and Christian understanding, Providence acts by contingent and indirect actions — events are not *fore*seen, because God doesn't "foresee" anything. He's not *before* and *after*, he's *present* to all things at one time. And like a great novelist, he sees the details of what he does and how they all hook together, without forcing anybody's liberty, without manipulating anything.

The early Americans who believed that the lifting of the fog on

Long Island was an act of God were not deists. Their God was not a "watchmaker God" who winds the universe up and lets it go. Their God cared about contingent affairs, loved particular nations, was interested in particular peoples and particular circumstances. Their God was the God of Judaism, the God of Providence. Not a swallow falls in the field but this God knows of it. His action is in the details.

TRUE LIBERTY: REFLECTION & CHOICE

When Jefferson wrote the Declaration of Independence he mentioned God twice. Before Congress would sign it, members insisted on two more references to God. Thus, these four names: the *Author* "of nature and nature's laws;" the *Creator* who endowed in us our rights; the *Judge* to whom we appeal in witness that our motives spring not out of seditiousness, but from a dear love of liberty and a deep sense of our own proper dignity; and *Providence*, a trust in divine Providence.

The fundamental meaning of the Jewish, and later the Christian, Bible is that the axis of the universe is what happens in the interior of the human being. Every story in the Bible is a story of what happens in the arena of the human will. In one chapter King David is faithful to his Lord and in the next, not. And the suspense of every chapter is, What will humans choose next? Liberty is the reason God made the universe. He wanted one creature capable of recognizing that he had made all things, that the creation is good, and that he had extended his hand in friendship. He wanted at least one creature to be able — not as a slave but as a free woman or man — to *choose* to reciprocate his proffered friendship.

The members of Congress on July 2, 1776, were about to make

themselves liable to the charge of treason and to humiliate their children into the *n*th generation for being the descendants of traitors. They appealed to an objective world, and beyond the eyes of an objective world they appealed to the Supreme *Judge* for the rectitude of their intentions. They needed that reference to their *Judge* in the Declaration. And they wanted that reference to *Providence*, to declare that God is on the side of Liberty, and that those who trust in liberty will therefore prevail. Whatever the odds, Providence will see to it that they prevail.

When Jefferson wrote the Declaration of
Independence he mentioned God twice.
Yet before Congress would sign it, members insisted
on two more references to God.

Let me recall from one of the old American hymns words that reflect exactly this biblical vision. This world didn't just "happen" — it was created for a purpose, and that purpose is *liberty.*

> Our fathers' God! To Thee,
> Author of liberty,
> To Thee we sing.
> Long may our land be bright
> With freedom's holy light;
> Protect us by Thy might,
> Great God our king.

At the beginning of *The Federalist*, in the second paragraph, the author says this generation of Americans is called upon to decide for all time whether governments can be formed "through reflection and choice" or must "forever be formed through accident and force." That's what the Americans were called upon to decide: whether a government may be formed through *reflection* and *choice*.

They then faced the question, How do you institutionalize such a decision? By calling a constitutional convention and then having the agreed-upon text ratified in a manner that permits the whole people to participate in the decision. Can there be enough votes for something like that? Can people put aside their regional prejudices? Can they put aside their personal ambitions? Can they think about what's good for posterity?

Remember the ambitions of that moment. For example, many New Yorkers wanted New York to be a separate nation. It would have its own secretary of state, its own commander in chief, its own secretary of the treasury; distinguished families in New York would become ambassadors to the Court of St. James and to Paris and so forth. Such a dream might seem very attractive to some leading families, but would it be good for the country? If New York were to vote to become an independent nation, there could be no union between New England and the South. *Reflection* and *choice*, then, were the hinges of liberty. What Americans meant by *liberty* are those acts that are made from reflection and choice — the acts that we commit ourselves to when we have rationally reflected on the alternatives, when we understand the consequences. That's freedom.

Freedom is not doing what you *want* to do; freedom is doing what, after reflection, you know you *ought* to do. That's why early American thought has been summed up thus: "Confirm thy soul in self-control, Thy liberty in law." Freedom springs from self-government, after reflection and by calm deliberate choice.

But to have reflection and choice, you need people with enough *virtue* to have command of their passions. You need people, that is, with the *habits* that allow them to reflect, to take time to be dispassionate, to see consequences clearly, and then to make a choice based on commitment. None of us act that way all the time. But we do aspire to have at least sufficient virtue to live responsibly. For how can a people unable to govern their passions in their private lives possibly be able to practice self-government in their public lives? It doesn't compute. In short, freedom in a republic is not feasible without virtue.

George Washington said in his Farewell Address that most people are not going to have virtue or good habits *in the long* run without religion. And what he meant by that can be recited very simply. As Jews and Christians understand it, religion is not just a cold law; it is a relationship with a Person — a Person who knows even your secret thoughts. So religion adds a personal motive to the idea of virtue. In addition to that, this Judge sees you even when you're alone, even with the doors closed. This is a Judge who knows whether or not you paint the bottom of the chair. Republics depend on virtue that holds up under such tests. The founding generation often used the example of the well-known doctor in Massachusetts who, having been involved in an adultery, turned out also to be a British spy. A Republic cannot be made up of people who think they can do in secret what they wouldn't do in public.

This is why the founders thought that we must not believe that virtue can be maintained in the long run without religion. Our sons are going to forget about the Revolution, the founders expected; they're going to forget the suffering we went through. They're going to forget the frozen feet at Valley Forge, the gangrene and the hunger, the lack of pay and the despair. They're going to forget all that, and their grandchildren will tire of hearing it. There's a moral entropy in human affairs, such that even if a generation succeeds in reaching a very high moral level, it's almost impossible for the next generation and the one after it to maintain that level. A republic, therefore, has to fight moral entropy. That's why there will have to be a series of moral awakenings. The founders didn't see how that would happen without religious inspiration, beyond a merely utilitarian impulse.

So, to repeat, there are three principles in this fundamental logic:

No republic without liberty; no liberty without virtue; no virtue without religion. Now doesn't that sound old-fashioned? These days, it hardly sounds tenable. Yet our founders may have been right. Is not our present circumstance dangerous to the Republic?

Freedom is always the most precarious regime. Even a single generation can throw it all away. Every generation must reflect and choose. As Dr. Joseph Warren, later killed at Bunker Hill, told the men of Massachusetts at Lexington: "Our country is in danger now, but not to be despaired of. On you depend the fortunes of America. You are to decide the important questions upon which rest the happiness and the liberty of millions not yet born. Act worthy of yourselves."

ADAPTED FROM THE TRANSCRIPT OF AN AFTER-DINNER SPEECH
GIVEN AT THE HOOVER INSTITUTION, OCTOBER 25, 1999

DISCUSSION
QUESTIONS

CHAPTER I – Faith, Friends, and Funds

Questions for Consideration:

1. How can friends help us see opportunities?

2. How can faith influence decision making?

3. Why is it important to have clear criteria for selecting stocks?

4. Socially Responsible Funds lack clear investing parameters. Why is this a problem?

CHAPTER 2 – The Heart of the Matter

Questions for Consideration:

1. Why is it important to know how and where our money is invested?

2. How do our investments affect who we are and who we become?

3. The author says, "happiness consists in living a life of integrity." What does this mean?

4. From the perspective of the Ave Maria Mutual Funds, what is the heart of the matter?

CHAPTER 3 – A Lifetime Preparing

Questions for Consideration:

1. What role does one's education play in the formation of mind and heart?
2. Why is family important in forming character?
3. How might entrepreneurial activity strengthen faith, morals, and character?

CHAPTER 4 – Abortion

Questions for Consideration:

1. Why screen out companies that have anything to do with abortion?
2. Carl Anderson states that abortion is different from all other issues. How is abortion different?
3. Is there a tangible difference between a human being and a human person?

CHAPTER 5 – Pornography

Questions for Consideration:

1. Why screen out companies that have anything to do with pornography?
2. What do we know about pornography today that was not known at the time the Supreme Court ruled that pornography is protected by the First Amendment?
3. Is there a tangible difference between pornography

and obscenity?

4. How is pornography a public health threat?

CHAPTER 6 – Morally Responsible Investing

Questions for Consideration:

1. What is Morally Responsible Investing?
2. Discuss the following statements from this chapter:

   Morally Responsible Investing can only be morally responsible by having zero tolerance for abortion and total love for innocent unborn human beings, their mothers, and all impacted by abortion.

   It is time to provide equal protection for all. Indeed, it is time to restore constitutional order, reject abortion, and choose life.

3. What can we do to ensure our investments reflect our core beliefs?

CHAPTER 7 – Faith and Reason

Questions for Consideration:

1. Why is a combination of faith and reason important when investing?
2. What is reflexive judgment?
3. What is reflective judgment?

4. What is Value Investing?
5. What is the art behind Value Investing?

CHAPTER 8 – A Clear Principle of Wisdom

Questions for Consideration:

1. Why is the essence of maturity?
2. What is "a clear principle of wisdom" in the context of investing?
3. Discuss this statement:

"Value Investing is thoroughly grounded in the principle of ownership." What does this mean? Why is this important?

CHAPTER 9 – Good Returns

Questions for Consideration:

1. What is institutional investment research?
2. Why is institutional investment research important?
3. Discuss these statements:

"In the Morally Responsible Investing approach, value and values really are complimentary concepts."

"The good investment-management practices, good fundamental research of our team of analysts, and good execution of sound investment strategies must be counted as factors in the excellent performance."

CHAPTER 10 – From Many One

Questions for Consideration:

1. Why is it important to understand America's founding documents?
2. "America is the only nation in the world that is founded on a creed." What does this mean?
3. Why is socialism incompatible with human flourishing?
4. How is capitalism compatible with liberty and the pursuit of happiness?
5. Discuss the following statements:

Socialism's fundamental flaw flows from its failure to see the human person as made in the image and likeness of God, and thereby, made to be free to create, dream, produce, and cultivate rather than submit to government programs that ultimately undermine the dignity of the person and decimate the desire to grow in virtue.

Our happiness flows from the liberty to make good decisions and to persevere in faith. From this place of virtue, we gain greater appreciation for our nation's unofficial and official motto. We trust in God as we overcome obstacles, pursue goals, and celebrate that we are all in this together – we are from many one.

CHAPTER 11 – Sound Advice

Questions for Consideration:

1. What is the value of sound advice?

2. Discuss the following statements:

Morally Responsible Investing provides the peace of mind that comes from knowing that one's investments do not support pornography, abortion, Planned Parenthood, or stem cell research.

Our approach seeks to provide clients with above average returns through investments in entities that have strong business characteristics and below average risk.

2. How does the Catholic Advisory Board facilitate Morally Responsible Investing?

CHAPTER 12 – In Memoriam

Questions for Consideration:

1. Discuss the life and most inspiring qualities of Bowie Kuhn.

2. Discuss the life and most inspiring qualities of Phyllis Schlafly.

3. Discuss the life and most inspiring qualities of Michael Novak.

4. Discuss ways that you strive to inspire others.

CHAPTER 13 – The Best Way Forward

Questions for Consideration:

1. "A nation's moral life is the foundation of its culture."
   What does this mean?

2. Discuss the following statements:

   Ave Maria Mutual Funds' success is due in large part to its philosophy – one that puts equal weight on investment performance and pro-life, pro-family values.

   With the prospect of being rewarded for excellence, a market economy incentivizes the production of quality products, optimal services, and reasonable prices.

   Investments require a free enterprise system and a free enterprise system can only thrive in the context of democratic capitalism rooted in eternal principles of justice and overseen by a government with checks and balances and a society steeped in virtue.

3. Which branch of government is least willing to operate within the scope of authority granted to it under the Constitution?

4. How do strong families and rigorous schools impact the health of nation?

Periods ended 6/30/2018	ONE YEAR	THREE YEARS*	FIVE YEARS*	TEN YEARS*	SINCE INCEPTION	GROSS/NET EXPENSE RATIO
Ave Maria Value Fund (Inception date 5-1-01)	15.90%	6.08%	6.73%	7.04%	6.98%	1.21%/1.21%
Ave Maria Growth Fund (Inception date 5-1-03)	20.54%	12.88%	13.68%	11.13%	11.30%	0.97%/0.97%
Ave Maria Rising Dividend Fund (Inception date 5-2-05)	12.70%	9.20%	10.55%	10.56%	9.25%	0.93%/0.93%
Ave Maria World Equity Fund (Inception date 4-30-10)	6.79%	6.34%	7.35%	-	7.08%	1.42%/1.26%
Ave Maria Bond Fund (Inception date 5-1-03)	2.19%	2.90%	3.03%	4.20%	4.07%	0.50%/0.50%

*Annualized

Performance data quoted represents past performance, which is no guarantee of future results. Investment return and principal value are historical and may fluctuate so that redemption value may be worth more or less than the original cost. Current performance may be lower or higher than what is quoted. Call 1-866-AVE-MARIA or visit www.avemariafunds.com for the most current month-end performance.

Request a prospectus, which includes investment objectives, risks, fees, expenses and other information that you should read and consider carefully before investing. The prospectus can be obtained by calling 1-866-283-6274 or it can be viewed at www.avemariafunds.com. Distributed by Ultimus Fund Distributors, LLC.

The adviser has contractually agreed to limit the ordinary operating expenses (excluding Acquired Fund Fees and Expenses, interest, taxes, brokerage costs and extraordinary expenses) of the Ave Maria World Equity Fund to and amount not exceeding 1.25% of the Fund's average daily net assets until at least May 1, 2019.

The Ave Maria Bond Fund's top ten holdings as of 6-30-18: U.S. Treasury Note 1.375% due 12/31/18 (3.1%), U.S. Treasury Note 1.50% due 10/31/19 (3.1%), U.S. Treasury Note 2.00% due 07/31/20 (1.6%), Texas Instruments, Inc. (1.6%), U.S. Treasury Note 1.875% due 02/28/22 (1.5%), U.S. Treasury Note 1.75% due 04/30/22 (1.5%), U.S Treasury Note 1.75% due 05/31/22 (1.5%), Royal Dutch Shell Spon ADR – B (1.4%), United Parcel Service, Inc. (1.3%) and Genuine Parts Company (1.3%). The Ave Maria Growth Fund's top ten holdings as of 6-30-18: Mastercard, Inc. (4.2%), O'Reilly Automotive, Inc. (4.1%), Rockwell Automation, Inc. (4.0%), Accenture PLC (4.0%), Copart, Inc. (3.7%), Visa, Inc. - Class A (3.5%), Medtronic PLC (3.4%), Moody's Corporation (3.3%), Lowe's Companies, Inc. (3.0%) and The Charles Schwab Corp. (2.8%). The Ave Maria Rising Dividend Fund's top ten holdings as of 6-30-18: Medtronic PLC (3.8%), Cognizant Tech. Solutions Corp. (3.7%), Lowe's Companies, Inc. (3.6%), RPM International, Inc. (3.5%), Tractor Supply Company (3.5%), TJX Companies, Inc. (3.5%), Diageo PLC ADR (3.4%), United Parcel Service, Inc. (3.4%), Zimmer Biomet Holdings, Inc. (3.3%) and Hexcel Corporation (3.2%). The Ave Maria Value Fund's top ten holdings as of 6-30-18: Texas Pacific Land Trust (7.0%), HEICO Corporation – Class A (4.7%), InterXion Holding NV (3.9%), Qurate Retail, Inc. (3.7%), American Airlines Group, Inc. (3.4%), Spectrum Brands Holdings, Inc. (3.2%), Arrow Electronics, Inc. (3.1%), Liberty Media Corp. Series C (2.9%), AMERCO (2.8%) and Noble Energy, Inc. (2.8%). The Ave Maria World Equity Fund's top ten holdings as of 6-30-18: Royal Dutch Shell Sponsored ADR – B (4.2%), Lowe's Companies, Inc. (3.7%), Medtronic PLC (3.6%), Mondelez International, Inc. (3.5%), Eaton Corporation (3.5%), The Chubb Corporation (3.5%), Panasonic Corporation (3.5%), Coca-Cola European Partners (3.4%), Zimmer Biomet Holdings, Inc. (3.1%) and AXA SA (3.1%). The most current available data regarding portfolio holdings can be found on our website, www.avemariafunds.com.

The Dow Jones Industrial Average is a price-weighted average of 30 significant stocks traded on the New York Stock Exchange and the NASDAQ. The S&P 500® Index is a capitalization weighted unmanaged index of 500 widely traded stocks, created by Standard & Poor's. The index is considered to represent the performance of the stock market in general. The Russell 3000® is a market-capitalization-weighted equity index maintained by the FTSE Russell that provides exposure to the entire U.S. stock market. The index tracks the performance of the 3,000 largest U.S.-traded stocks which represent about 98% of all U.S incorporated equity securities. You cannot invest directly in an index.

Schwartz Investment Counsel, Inc., a registered investment adviser established in 1980, serves as investment adviser for Ave Maria Mutual Funds. The Adviser invests in securities only if they meet the Funds' investment and religious requirements, and as such, the returns may be lower or higher than if the Adviser made decisions based solely on investment considerations. The Funds' method of security selection may or may not be successful and the Funds may underperform or outperform the stock market as a whole. All mutual funds are subject to market risk, including possible loss of principal. The Funds' investments in small and mid capitalization companies could experience greater volatility than investments in large capitalization companies. AVEWX invests in foreign securities and securities issued by U.S. entities with substantial foreign operations. Investments in these securities can involve additional risks relating to political, economic or regulatory conditions in foreign countries. These risks include less stringent investor protection and disclosure standards of some foreign markets; fluctuations in foreign currencies; and withholding or other taxes. AVEFX invests primarily in fixed income securities and as a result the Fund is also subject to the followings risks: interest rate risk, credit risk, credit rating risk, prepayment and extension risk and liquidity risk.

The discussion of the performance of the Ave Maria Mutual Funds (the "Funds") is designed to set forth my views of the market and to provide a discussion of the investment strategies used by the investment adviser in managing each Fund's assets.

Any listing or discussion of specific securities is intended to help the reader understand a Fund's investment strategies and/or factors that may influence a Fund's investment performance, and should not be regarded as a recommendation of any security. I believe there is a reasonable basis for any opinions expressed, although actual results may differ, sometimes significantly so, from those I expect and express herein. Statements referring to future actions or events, such as the future financial performance or ongoing business strategies of the companies in which a Fund invests, are based on the current expectations and projections about future events provided by various sources, including company management. These statements are not guarantees of future performance, and actual events and results may differ materially from those discussed herein.

Any opinions and views expressed related to the prospects of any individual portfolio holdings or grouping thereof or of a Fund itself are "forward looking statements" which may or may not prove to be accurate over the long term when viewed from the perspective of hindsight. Future results or performance cannot be assured. You should not place undue reliance on forward looking statements, which are effective only as of the date this material is published.

References to securities purchased or held are only as of the date published. Although the Funds' investment adviser focuses on long-term investments, holdings are subject to change.

My comments are influenced by my analysis of information from a wide variety of sources and may contain syntheses, synopses, or excerpts of ideas from written or oral viewpoints provided to me by investment, industry, press and other public sources about various economic, political, central bank, and other suspected influences on investment markets.

INDEX

A

abortion..........................3, 8, 11, 13, 22, 33, 41-42, 53-60, 62-66, 69-71, 78, 84-85, 89-91, 103, 127, 130, 140, 165, 184, 192, 202, 212, 220, 226, 229, 238-239, 254-255, 258

advertising...................................27-28, 30, 67, 137

American Express.....................................141, 239

Anchoring 114

Apple 150, 199

Arroyo, Raymond 32, 194

Ave Maria Bond Fund...........7, 164-165, 201, 260

Ave Maria Catholic Values Fund 7, 26-27, 31, 35, 139, 164

Ave Maria Growth Fund.............. 7, 164, 166, 260

Ave Maria Mutual Funds.................1, 3-4, 6-7, 18, 22, 29-33, 35, 64, 84-85, 103, 131, 135, 137, 139, 161-162, 164, 166, 194, 196, 198, 201, 207-209, 218, 220-221, 229, 235, 238, 253, 259, 261

Ave Maria Radio 1, 16

Ave Maria Rising Dividend Fund.................7, 164, 166, 260

Ave Maria University 1, 16, 205, 218

Ave Maria Value Fund 7, 164, 166, 260

Ave Maria World Equity Fund 7, 164-165, 260

B

baseball 3, 10, 13, 15, 17-18, 32, 208-209

Behavioral Finance 114, 116

Berkshire Hathaway 130, 140-141, 152, 239

Buffett, Warren...........62, 106, 110, 117, 130, 140, 142-143, 147, 154, 156, 239

Burlington Northern Santa Fe 141

C

capitalism... 92, 105, 171, 173-174, 178-179, 181, 183-186, 188-189, 191, 197, 215-216, 218, 222, 227, 240, 257, 259

Caritas in Veritate 241

Catholic Advisory Board 6, 8, 24, 33, 83, 92, 132, 134, 163, 165, 167, 171, 186, 195, 202, 204, 206-207, 209, 212, 214, 236, 258

Catholic Church 6, 8, 35, 53, 62, 67, 69, 82, 94, 139, 165, 202-203, 209, 214, 221

Catholic Values Investment Trust 10

Centesimus Annus.......................................93, 217

Christ 37, 94, 100, 161, 205, 229

Christian 41, 48, 50, 93, 167, 243, 247-248

Christianity.............................. 124, 230, 237, 242

Churchill, Winston...........................181-182, 189

Clerestory Communications 28

CNBC.. 30

Coca-Cola............................... 142, 147-148, 260

commissions...26-27

communism 75, 77-79, 82, 94, 102, 179-180

Congress...........61, 69, 83, 112, 170-171, 221, 225, 244-249

Constitution.................. 41-42, 60-61, 68, 95, 177, 187-190, 221, 223-227, 240, 259

Creator 56, 78, 169-170, 243, 248

culture......................13, 33, 56, 65-66, 68-69, 71, 75, 81, 84, 86, 89-91, 94, 171, 173-174, 190-191, 215-216, 220, 223, 228, 236-237, 259

D

Declaration of Independence.............. 61, 169, 171, 189-190, 220, 240, 243, 248

Democrats........................... 183, 191, 195, 197, 215

Detroit.................. 1, 13-15, 23, 26, 36-37, 40, 43, 46-48, 50, 125, 127, 132, 159, 205-206

Detroit Tigers 1, 13

discipline......... 37-38, 40, 116, 120, 193, 231, 236

diversification..116

Dominican Sisters of Mary 17

Domino's.................... 1, 3, 13-16, 23, 29, 132, 204

Domino's Farms 14, 132, 204

E

EBITDA 147

economic........... 8, 24, 89, 92-93, 95-97, 104, 109, 114, 120, 132, 150-151, 170, 172-173, 178-181, 186-189, 191, 205, 214-215, 228, 230-231, 233, 236-237, 261

economy...................................... 93-96, 113, 151, 170, 179, 185-186, 188-189, 191, 194-195, 198, 222-223, 227-228, 230-233, 238, 241, 259

education........................10, 24, 36, 38, 40, 43-44, 56, 66, 74, 89, 127, 183, 190-191, 254

embryonic stem cell research.................... 24, 103, 165, 192, 202

England...............138, 171-172, 181, 191, 222, 250

Enterprise Value (EV)...............................104, 147

entrepreneurial............. 36, 46, 124, 129, 171, 254

entrepreneurs 125, 172-173, 222

entrepreneurship.................................17, 46, 185

environment............................ 103, 186, 223, 233

equity 7, 16, 72, 147, 150, 152, 164-165, 201, 232, 234, 260-261

EWTN.................................17-18, 32-33, 66, 90, 105, 132, 194, 205

F

federal 62, 67, 69, 91, 112, 123, 139, 175, 177, 188, 223, 227

fiduciary....................................2, 27, 102, 162, 193

finance............. 15, 50, 92, 114, 116, 150, 160, 188

financial 5, 8, 34, 50-51, 66, 99, 102-104, 107-108, 112, 114, 120, 134, 138, 140, 150-151, 153, 156-158, 160, 162, 167, 177, 188, 199-200, 233, 238, 261

foundation 10, 23-24, 49, 53, 66, 78, 132, 177, 191, 204-205, 220, 223, 226, 228-231, 259

founder............................ 3, 15, 23, 72, 160, 194

founders 187, 224-225, 243, 246, 251-252

Franklin, Benjamin 170

Free Cash Flow 150

freedom.......................... 69, 77, 83, 85-87, 89, 92, 99, 171, 177, 179, 213, 221-222, 227-228, 249-252

fundamentals...............................95, 98, 114, 170

fundamental security analysis 166, 193

G

gambling... 136, 160

General Motors.......................................112, 149

George, Robert P. 83, 132, 204, 229

German..29, 40, 49, 137

Germany... 39, 129, 181

Good Returns 2-3, 135, 161, 186, 256

goodwill...145-147

government.............................7, 24-26, 39, 61-62, 95, 111-112, 138-139, 149, 165, 173-175, 177, 180, 182, 184-191, 197-198, 221-225, 227-228, 231, 239-241, 250, 257, 259

H

Hahn, Scott 132, 204

happiness............................34, 51, 170, 185, 187, 190, 213, 220, 229, 252-253, 257

Harvard.......................... 107, 116, 122, 210, 217

health 63, 73, 83, 85, 88-89, 171, 191, 227, 242-243, 255, 259

healthcare...158-159

heuristics...114, 123

Holtz, Lou...................... 3-4, 131-132, 134, 204

I

inflation 139, 233

invest..................................3, 5, 7-8, 10-12, 33, 65, 99, 104, 137, 158, 165, 195-196, 199-200, 222, 234-235, 238, 261

investors 3, 20, 24, 26-27, 30, 34-35, 51, 70, 101-102, 106-107, 109-112, 114-118, 120-122, 136-139, 141-142, 145, 149, 151-154, 156-157, 160-163, 171, 178, 195-196, 198, 220, 227, 229, 232-239, 261

J

justice...54-56, 59, 64, 69, 83, 90, 95, 98, 119, 169, 177, 185, 208, 221, 225-

226, 229-230, 240, 259

K

Kudlow, Larry.......... 24, 33-34, 131-132, 171, 191, 194-195, 205
Kuhn, Bowie...................... 1, 3, 10, 13, 17, 22-23, 30-34, 36, 131, 207, 218, 229, 258

L

Legatus...1, 15, 205
liberal............71, 92, 103, 140, 176, 195, 216, 219
liberalism 13, 71, 76-77, 88, 224, 241
liberty.........................51, 77, 83, 93, 95, 170-171, 179, 182, 185-187, 190, 215, 217, 220, 229, 243, 245-252, 257, 260
Lincoln, Abraham.....................70, 223, 228-229, 231, 241-242, 263
Liquidation Value (LV).....................143, 145-146

M

Magisterium.......................... 12, 20, 165, 167, 218
Major League Baseball........3, 10, 18, 32, 208-209
market.............................. 5, 9, 20, 73, 94-96, 106, 109-111, 113-114, 116-118, 120, 137, 139, 141-144, 146-157, 163, 165-166, 171, 185-186, 194-195, 197-200, 220, 222-223, 230-235, 241, 259, 261
marriage........ 19, 23, 56, 69, 88-89, 129, 174-176, 186-187, 190-191, 212-213, 220, 223, 228
Marxism...94, 216
Medicaid 62
Michigan....... 13, 16, 43, 49-50, 63, 128, 159, 192
Microsoft 115, 150
Monaghan, Thomas......................... 1, 3, 9, 13, 22, 25, 29, 32, 36, 131-132, 205, 207, 212, 229
Morally Responsible Investing (MRI)..............2-3, 6, 9, 24, 29-30, 32, 34, 41, 51, 53, 64, 70, 72, 89, 91, 94, 96, 98, 101, 129, 135, 161-162, 166, 168, 185-186, 192, 202-203, 207, 220, 227, 230, 236, 239-240, 255-256, 258
Moschella, Melissa................................... 132, 205
mutual funds............................ 1, 3-4, 6-8, 18, 22, 26-27, 29-33, 35, 64-65, 84-85, 102-103, 131, 135, 137, 139, 142, 160-162, 164, 166, 168, 192, 194, 196, 198-199, 201, 207-209, 218, 220-221, 229, 234-235, 238, 253, 259, 261

N

Net Present Value (NPV) 144-146
networks.. 210, 228
neuroeconomics................................ 107, 114, 123
Nihilism...................................... 77, 80, 82, 88
Novak, Michael 23, 92, 131, 133, 179-180, 185, 207, 215, 217-219, 222, 227, 229, 242, 258

O

Obama 78-79, 81, 88, 90-91, 95, 105, 112, 197, 236
Obama Administration 81, 197
obscenity 67-68, 75-76, 81, 88, 255
opportunities 5-6, 14, 20, 34, 50, 77, 84, 136-137, 143, 151, 159, 235, 253
opportunity...................... 3, 12-13, 22, 30, 33-35, 70, 110, 122, 142-143, 148, 154, 162, 173, 179, 185-186, 190, 192, 210, 222, 236
optimism...........................107, 158, 232-233, 237
ownership...............................93, 96-99, 101, 104, 142, 144, 170-171, 173, 180, 184-185, 215, 232, 256

P

parents.................38, 40-41, 43-44, 124, 129, 176
performance..................4, 101, 116, 137, 141, 150, 152, 155-156, 162, 166-168, 193, 221, 235, 256, 259-261
philosophy........................... 12, 15, 77, 79, 92, 94, 140, 154, 220, 228, 259
Planned Parenthood 22, 24, 53, 62-63, 66, 74-75, 90-91, 105, 140, 165, 192, 199, 202, 212, 220, 239, 258
Platte, Richard 235
Playboy Enterprises....................................... 71-72
political 26, 79-80, 82, 89, 103, 159, 164, 172, 181-184, 191, 204, 214-215, 223-225, 261
Pope Benedict XVI.............................. 8, 230, 241
Pope Leo XIII 93
Pope Pius XI 93
Pope Pius XII 136, 143, 156, 160
Pope Saint John Paul II...................85, 93-94, 106, 123, 217-218
pornography...................... 3, 8, 11, 13, 22, 24, 41, 67-76, 78, 81, 83-86, 88-89, 103, 174, 192, 202,

212, 220, 226-227, 229, 254-255, 258

Price/Earning (P/E) ratio.................... 84, 100-101, 104, 106, 114-115, 118, 141-144, 146-148, 152, 155, 182, 193, 200, 234

Private Market Value (PMV) 144

profession..116, 218

professional 4, 18, 20, 27, 31, 36, 50-51, 117, 130, 140, 158, 162-163, 193, 210

professor................ 43, 83, 92, 132, 204-205, 218

profit 9, 138, 150, 152-153, 156, 159, 172-173, 180, 206, 237

profits...............7, 62, 151, 172, 194-196, 198, 237

pro-life 4, 8, 11, 16, 20, 22-23, 33, 35, 41, 51, 63, 66, 161, 167, 221, 236, 238, 259

prospectus..23, 238, 260

Proxy Contest 101

psychology..107, 113, 116-117, 233

public relations.. 28, 103

Purvis, Gloria... 132, 205

Q

Quadragesimo Anno 93, 105

R

Reagan, Ronald 70, 94, 205, 264

religion 53, 71, 91, 94, 161, 217, 231, 237, 243, 245, 251-252

religious............................ 5, 10, 17, 23, 30, 32, 38, 70, 77, 90, 92, 117-120, 156, 162, 172, 177, 204, 231, 235, 242-243, 245, 252, 261

Republic..................... 216, 221, 242-243, 251-252

Republican.................................92, 187, 191, 227

Rerum Novarum 93, 105, 217

research 20, 24, 27, 34, 50, 91, 103, 109, 112-114, 117-118, 123, 137, 151, 157, 160, 163, 165, 167, 186, 192-193, 202, 256, 258

responsibility............................. 2, 9, 57, 102, 162, 171, 174, 193, 216, 237

Riccardo, Fr. John.................................... 132, 205

Roney, Paul 15, 23, 131-132, 204

S

Sanders, Bernie 95, 182-183, 191

Schlafly, Phyllis............23, 131, 133, 207, 210-211,

218-219, 227, 229, 236, 241, 258

Schwartz Investment Counsel, Inc................. 1, 3, 15, 27, 84, 163, 192, 194, 204, 261

Schwartz Value Fund............................. 26-27, 50

securities 7, 9, 22, 139, 149, 154, 165-166, 231, 261

Securities and Exchange Commission (SEC)....22, 139

security analysis 154-157, 166, 193

shareholder......................... 135, 151, 160-161, 239

socialism 75, 93, 95, 102, 105, 172-175, 177-181, 183-185, 187, 189-190, 215-216, 227, 257

stock market meltdown 109

stocks 7, 11-12, 104, 110, 114-116, 118-119, 137, 142, 146, 148, 154-155, 164, 167, 196, 199, 201, 221, 232-234, 238, 241, 253, 261

Supreme Court 41-42, 55, 59, 67-71, 91, 212, 224, 226, 254

T

Thomas More Law Center 16

Trump................................ 191, 194, 197-198, 231

Tulip Mania 111

unborn 1, 13, 17, 41-42, 54-55, 58-59, 61-64, 90-91, 208, 212, 255

U

Unique Proprietary Position (UPP).................148

United States.............. 42, 54-56, 58-59, 63, 67, 69, 71-72, 76, 78, 90, 94, 105, 170-173, 175, 177-179, 182-183, 187, 189, 213, 221-223, 228, 240

V

Value Investing....................................27, 106, 115, 139-143, 150, 154, 160, 166, 232, 256

values..7, 10-11, 17, 26-28, 31, 35, 97, 99, 101, 124, 137, 139-140, 152, 164-166, 221, 234, 236, 256, 259

Virginia 18, 85, 209, 244

virtue.....................................48, 70, 161, 174, 181, 186, 189-191, 208, 228, 240, 244-245, 251-252, 257, 259

W

Wall Street Journal...........................32, 71, 88, 94,

  96, 105, 107, 155

Walmart 115, 141, 148-149

Washington 18, 22, 37, 49, 64,
  70, 205, 210, 242, 244, 246-247, 251

wealth 95, 97, 99, 111, 117,
  173, 188-189, 232

Weigel, George 218, 229

Wells Fargo 141, 153